A Harvest of Memories

Farming Reflections On Times Gone By

A story by D. Jeffers

Sketches by artist Ian Scott

Note for Librarians: A cataloguing record for this book is available from Library and Archives Canada at www.collectionscanada.ca/amicus/index-e.html

ISBN 1-4251-0522-X

Printed in Victoria, BC, Canada. Printed on paper with minimum 30% recycled fibre. Trafford's print shop runs on "green energy" from solar, wind and other environmentally-friendly power sources.

Offices in Canada, USA, Ireland and UK

Book sales for North America and international:
Trafford Publishing, 6E–2333 Government St.,
Victoria, BC V8T 4P4 CANADA
phone 250 383 6864 (toll-free 1 888 232 4444)
fax 250 383 6804; email to orders@trafford.com
Book sales in Europe:
Trafford Publishing (UK) Limited, 9 Park End Street, 2nd Floor
Oxford, UK OX1 1HH UNITED KINGDOM
phone +44 (0)1865 722 113 (local rate 0845 230 9601)
facsimile +44 (0)1865 722 868; info.uk@trafford.com
Order online at:
trafford.com/06-2280

10 9 8 7 6 5 4 3 2

Preface

The seeds of 'long ago' were in my head for a long time before they started to sprout. At long last they have grown to maturity and now I have eventually gathered them into 'A Harvest of Memories'.

It is an attempt to put on record an era which has passed, before it is lost forever. Hopefully future generations and historians will find merit in my efforts. It was not an easy life by any standards and working conditions were tough; kids went bare footed to school, and poverty was obvious. Today, men and women jointly work to pay the mortgage, in bygone times, they worked together on the land to help put bread on the table and if there was anything to spare footwear for their children, and maybe a little Christmas surprise!

But there was another side to life too; community spirit did exist and the more fortunate helped the less fortunate. There was also, of course, that delightful sense of humour, which we Irish are endowed with, and manys the practical joke was played on man or woman, and the only damage done was to the pride of the recipient!

My thanks to the late Myles Fleming, and Joe Brown, also Joe Byrne, for some of the stories that kick started me into action, making the effort to record them before forgotten for all time. I must also thank Michael Ward, retired editor of the Ballymore Bugle, and Pastor Robert Dunlop, for painstakingly reading and correcting the stories, and keeping up the pressure to try and galvanise me into action. My brother Derek in

California also played a part in that exercise! Many thanks to Ian Scott for his artwork, every picture tells a story we're told and his sketches do just that. Mairead McGuinness and Philip Lynch must also get a mention for their fulsome words about 'A Harvest of Memories'. These are two people with that 'get up and go' attitude that Philip refers to in his foreword; both in their own way putting Ireland up there with the best of them though coming at it from different angles.

These stories are dedicated to my Father and Mother who struggled through the Hungry Thirties and somehow managed to give their three children a good education enabling us to appreciate rural living in spite of it's hardships, and also appreciate that there was more to living than just 'mullacan and mulen'. Dick Jeffers.

Foreword

Dick Jeffers' book "A Harvest of Memories" is as charming as its author. The details of country life are relayed in a gentle, easy style—but the harsh moments of ordinary life are also vividly recounted. Like the hardships experienced by the farm labourer's wife, struggling on a pittance to provide food, clothes and heat for the family.

Each chapter reveals a facet of life from Dick's passage through time and through a changing farming landscape. Thanks to this book, I now know exactly what the Select Vestry does! This is just one of the gentle nuggets of information I have gleaned from "A Harvest of Memories". There are many, many more.

It is a great tribute to Dick that he has taken the time to write down his special memories, so that others will appreciate that there was a time before the Celtic Tiger took hold. He recalls a kind, but also cruel place, that banished single mothers. Politicians get honourable and dishonourable mention too! Not forgetting Brussels bureaucrats and revenue collectors. Few escape, which is as it should be in any harvest, where everything is gathered in.

Mairead McGuinness MEP

Memories, it is said, are as fresh as freshly cut grass.

We are all conditioned and moulded by those around us in our earliest years. These are the influences that never leave us and when I first read ' A Harvest of Memories' by Dick Jeffers I could not avoid going back in time and vividly picturing life as it was then.

Dick's level of recall and descriptive powers combine to provide the reader with a thoroughly entertaining and captivating 'read' that will fascinate older readers who can identify with the Ireland of their earlier years and, equally importantly, and hugely informative for young readers who have no concept of a home life without water or power, fridge or television...

When one reads remarks such as "piped water was unheard of..." and "the odd house had a wireless set" you come to swiftly realise that the other Ireland in which many of us grew up was not so long ago.

Growing up in the 1930s was challenging for parents making ends meet. Money was scarce and neighbours pooled their resources and helped each other, especially during the harvest season. Quoting Dick, those working in the fields were sustained by "soda bread, liberally coated with jam, and all washed down with strong tay." The great sense of community is superbly summed up by the following: "You can live without your relatives, but you can't live without your neighbours."

The past, somehow, always seems shrouded in a golden glow but let no one forget, and Dick certainly doesn't, that people endured hard times when work dominated life and leisure time was little.

There are many wonderful anecdotes in this book...personal stories that capture the economic, social and cultural climate of the time. And morbid as it may sound, 'The Wake' is an engaging chapter, gently laced with humour. More importantly, however, are the lessons inherent in Dick's book.

In particular, this book deals with the era which preceded the dramatic uplift in our economic fortunes but the reader can grasp the tenacity, the drive and the commitment of that generation to sow the seeds of a 'get up and go' attitude in their children. Truly, those people were the mothers and fathers of our economic success.

'A Harvest of Memories' is a delightfully engaging book.

Philip Lynch, C.E.O. One 51 plc.

Contents

Chapter 1 15
The Boss Man - Introduces my father and mother. If it wasn't for them I wouldn't have been around to write these stories!

Chapter 2 21
Growing up a Protestant - Is mostly about growing up as a small boy in a Protestant culture in Ireland.

Chapter 3 33
The Hungry Thirties - A brief explanation of the Hungry Thirties abroad and at home, also explains why the shortage of money in olden times didn't prevent people from living and enjoying themselves in spite of its absence!

Chapter 4 47
Hitler's War - How it benefited Ireland. Emigrant's money being sent home, and the opportunity to work, which was unavailable at home.

Chapter 5 51
War and Horses - During the war years horses of all kinds were in big demand and gave my Father the opportunity to show his mettle.

Chapter 6 63
The Dismal Fifties - We break away from Thirties thinking, but progress is slow!

Chapter 7 71
EEC - Entry to Europe and consequent benefits.

Chapter 8 77
The Fordson Tractor - Irelands first approach to mechanisation, and how it was adopted wholeheartedly by the farm worker.

Chapter 9 87
The Ferguson TE 20 - This tractor was the turning point in mechanised farming, but it took a while to sell itself to 'Doubtful Thomas's' in the farming fraternity.

Chapter 10 91
The Reaper and Binder - The half way stage between backbreaking work in the harvest field, and today's modern combine harvester.

Chapter 11 97
Thrashing - Sweat, dust, and rat killing, and the hazards faced on road and in haggard when moving from farm to farm.

Chapter 12 105
The Agriculture Contractor - Very much in vogue today, but was always there in bygone times as additional farm income.

Chapter 13 111
Neighbours - How to, and how not to, get along with them, and their real worth in times of trouble or need.

Chapter 14 123
A Settin' of Eggs - A settin' of eggs relates how important the money earned from selling eggs was to the farmer's wife, and how it doesn't pay to get too greedy.

Chapter 15 131
Pin Money - Many of today's women, married or single, are financially independent and what they earn could hardly be described as 'pin money'. Yesterday's rural woman struggled hard for her independence, be it selling eggs, butter, the odd calf or piglet, or thinning roots for farmers and cutting sheaves at thrashing time. Bord Failte and the B@B's set her up and gave some the chance to earn real money.

Chapter 16 137

Daisy the House Cow - Queen of the farmyard, her welfare was important not only to the farmer and his family but various other farm animals. Her yearly journey to a suitor is recorded

Chapter 17 145

Sheep - A law unto themselves, and the bane of all owners when any form of control is practiced. The buying and selling of them is an art form.

Chapter 18 155

Fairs Old and New - The period covered is from the old hand spittin' an' clappin' fair green days, to the modern Livestock auction ring. The Dealin' Man was PR personified!

Chapter 19 169

The Training of the Collie Pup - The Collie Pup and how he should not be trained.

Chapter 20 175

The Rescue of Kelpie - A favourite sheepdog who was lost and was rescued.

Chapter 21 179

The Farm Labourer - His trials and tribulations. Low wages and long hours usually carried with a cheerful disposition.

Chapter 22 191

The Farm Labourers Wife - The same trials only female. The options of the single girl were limited. The best was made of a bad lot.

Chapter 23 201

The County Show - All the hoopla of preparation, then disappointment when honour is called into question.

Chapter 24 207
The Gunner Ryan - A dacent man not over fond of work, but needs must when the Devil drives. Prayers to our Lady are of little help.

Chapter 25 213
The Campaign - Harvesting sugar beet, the exact opposite of grain harvesting. Mud, mud, and more mud.

Chapter 26 219
T'will Do Well Enough - Exactly what it says, and putting it on the long finger only makes matters worse.

Chapter 27 229
The Wake - We're a nation of funeral goers, and the Wake still holds a respected position in rural Ireland.

Chapter 28 235
Idle Thoughts - Reflections on many aspects of farming and rural living down through the years.

Chapter 1

The Boss Man

Born and raised on a farm in the "Thirties" I have endeavoured to put together a combination of observations and events that have taken place from that time onwards. Central to those early years was the Boss Man (my father), an irascible and quirky character whose influence, not only on the immediate family, but also on the neighbourhood is worth remembering. Of independent mind he recognised neither class, creed, or colour and had a healthy distain for politics. Put another way, he was a law onto himself All were equal in his eyes provided you measured up to his criteria for assessment; could you carry out the job allotted to you to his satisfaction? If so, you were on a winner. At busy times he often employed 'casual labour'; some of them carrying baggage, or to put it in Irish terms 'they would lift the cross iv an' asses back'; eggs, a spade, or anything that wasn't nailed down. My father would overlook this little foible if the person employed was a good worker. Of course there were times when he and some neighbour didn't see eye to eye. It was usually over broken fences or stock straying. He would blow up instantly; tell the neighbour in a few succinct words what he thought of him and storm off. By the next day it was all forgotten as far as he was concerned. He never held a grudge.

To understand the man better a dip into his background might be a help. I never knew my grandparents on his side of the family. Neither did he. Both his parents died when he was very young. Coming from a large family he was shipped out to a fond uncle for rearing. That worked fine until the uncle's wife died and he married again. The new bride and my father apparently didn't see eye to eye so he packed what belongings he had and moved across the fields to another family. They took him in and there he stayed until he got the itch to travel. His education was brief for he fell foul of his teacher by standing up in class, throwing a slate at him and marching out the door. His travels took him to Canada, a new developing country. In this new country he developed his first and last passion; his love of horses. Horse wrangler, bronco buster, horse trainer and owner, he criss - crossed the country and the United States going from racetrack to racetrack with a considerable degree of success. After twelve years abroad he returned home and married the pick of the basket of a Scotch Presbyterian family, my mother.

A loving, gentle, woman, she was the anchor to this rather impetuous man.

He was 'an early riser'. By the time the workers came in at eight o'clock in the morning he would have the horses fed, tackled, and standing out in the yard ready for action. When later he acquired a tractor (the first in the parish) it would be fuelled, checked, and also ready for action. It was said of him that he 'had a day's work done before anyone else got to thinking about it'. He also owned a motor car, an Austin Tourer, used very little during the week, but taken out on Sundays to take the family to church.

As I've already stated my father didn't pull his punches regardless of whom or what he was addressing. He was a member of the Select Vestry and there from time to time he locked horns with the ruling autocracy of the day. I should explain that a Select Vestry is a committee formed to keep an eye on the three F's. The furnishings, fabrics, and most important, the finances, of each Church of Ireland parish. The prevailing Rector is always the Chairman. It is a democratic body with all elected members having their say, but in my fathers time it was probably more autocratic than democratic. This was probably due to a number of factors. People were maybe not so well educated; the clergy were held in high esteem and greatly respected, anyone holding a military rank or title (the two went together very often) was also held in awe. In essence one could say, that the workings of the vestry were governed by the Chairman (rector) and anyone who carried rank or title, all others were 'yes men'. This situation did not go down well with a man of independent temperament such as my father, especially when financial matters were under review. The Rector at the time he trusted implicitly with the souls of the parish, but not the finances. The man carrying rank, a retired army major, he had little time for, saying, with great disregard for all such personnel, that service men were incapable of making decisions because someone else from higher up made them for them. He obviously didn't think much of those in high places either, for he often remarked to my mother after a marathon vestry meeting that it was a source of amazement to him as to how the Allies won the war.

But times move on. World War 2 had come to an end, the rector in question got kicked upstairs, a new one was appointed, and the Major sold up and moved. Oddly enough, a new Major took his place on the vestry. This new fellow was a bit of a diplomat and knew how to handle men, and that included my Father. They got on well together inside and outside of vestry meetings! This change of heart on my Father's behalf was probably due to a combination of things. Maybe he was mellowing as the years caught up with him, the Major's charm may have had an effect, but I suspect the bond that cemented the friendship was the love of horses that both men had. Hunting and racing was meat and drink to the pair of them. They did spar at times at vestry meetings, but my Father gave up wondering how the Allies won the war!

One couldn't finish writing about my Father without a mention of my Mother. A kind gentle woman she was the exact opposite of him. Opposites attract they say and so it was in their case. He always seemed to have several balls in the air at one and the same time with nobody knowing which one he was going to run with. I often wonder did he know himself. There's no doubt but she was the anchor in the marriage, and although he usually paid scant attention to what others thought, in matters important he listened to her and took heed.

She started off in her young life with ambitions to be a

children's nurse, but then my Father got in the way! Nevertheless her social conscience stayed with all her life, especially where young children were concerned. If she heard of an ailing child, especially among the poorer people who lived around us she was off with a two pound jar of blackcurrant jam A hot blackcurrant drink was the 'cure all' for sore throats, snotty noses, and most minor ailments in small children in those days. Come Christmas a large Rhode Island Red cockerel, fattened to the gills would find its way into the same houses, compliments of my Mother.

If horses were my Father's passion hers was gardening. I guess that's where the seemingly endless supply of blackcurrant jam came from, for come fruit picking time all were rounded up to lend a hand. We had a large walled in garden that had seen better times. We kids fought with nettles and briars to get at the raspberries and currants but it did contain all the essential fruits and vegetables to keep a household going for most of the year. At slack times on the farm, either between hoeing and haying, or haying and harvesting, a man was put into the garden to do the heavy spade work, and attempt to keep the briars at bay with a slash-hook. A Shanks hand pushed lawnmower kept the grass borders!

Chapter 2

Growing up a Protestant

So how have we, a Protestant farming family, fitted in all down the years with our Roman Catholic neighbours. The short answer is—well. History will relate how there was a certain Catholic triumphalism at the start of Independence which lasted certainly through the reign of Archbishop John Charles McQuaid, and I suppose small blame to them, for the shoe was on the other foot for long enough. There was the Fethard –on –Sea boycott, the ban on a Protestant lady getting a job as County Librarian, the Ne Temere decree, the GAA ban, and not forgetting 'the special position of the Roman Catholic Church'! But all of this stuff was way over the head of a small boy growing up in rural Ireland, and later on when playing rugby for a provincial club, we had a fellow who played rugby with us on Saturday and played GAA on Sunday. The fact that he sneaked through the hedge and joined us just before kick off must have had some significance! It was also over the heads of neighbours when help was needed to get up a field of hay, help out at a thrashing, or more important, helping out when trouble or sickness threatened. Lay folk and clergy of all persuasions today make a big deal out of ecumenism and that's good, but it was always there in farming circumstances, we just didn't have a name for it. Chatting with a neighbour over the hedge on a fine spring day, or giving a hand out when help was short, made up for any difference there may have been between the two denominations. Differences there were, but each side to a large degree respected them.

Ironically, there were subtle differences between the various Protestant denominations, Church of Ireland, Presbyterians, Methodists, Baptists, in those long ago times. Theological speaking, I suppose these differences were ones of interpretation of the 'Word', but in reality, it was only a case of tu'pence halfpenny looking down on tu'pence. The Church of Ireland considered itself the senior party of the various Protestant denominations! My Father and Mother crossed the divide for their marriage was a 'mixed marriage' of sorts; my Mother came from a Scots Presbyterian family. A generation down the road and yours truly did likewise, for my wife came from a strong Methodist family! So you could say we were and are a crazy mixed up bunch! Nowadays it doesn't matter a hap'orth, and to be honest it didn't make much difference then, but the real 'mixed marriage', Protestant/Catholic was a cause for concern amongst Protestant denominations, for the Ne Temere decree ruled, and adherence to it decimated the Protestant population. I guess the decree is still on the statue books of the Roman Catholic faith, but no one pays it a mite of attention today.

The uninitiated might be forgiven for thinking, that, that

grand sounding name, Protestant Church Social Party was a political party. It was nothing of the sort. In fact it was nothing more than a dance, held monthly in Protestant parish halls, usually the Protestant school, around the country. The concept was to raise parish funds, always in short supply, but there was an underlying reason also! At the time it was the hope of all mummies and daddies that their much loved siblings would have the opportunity to meet their opposites within the confines of the parish social. It was by 'invitation only', which was a polite way of saying, "all others keep out". It was the 'Ballroom of Romance' days. The girls were the first arrivals, laden down with plates of sandwiches and cakes, for dancing was hungry work. It was also an opportunity for a girl to show off her culinary assets should the man of her desires be in attendance that night. In a close knit community it wasn't too difficult to suss out who made what! With the grub all laid out in readiness the women took up their positions on one side of the hall, chatting, gossiping, and waited for the men folk to arrive. Pub closing hours was the signal for the arrival of the men; a bit of Dutch courage didn't go astray, especially if a lad was a bit on the shy side when asking a girl to take the floor with him, and he maybe with two left feet! The 'city slicker', young men sent by head office to work in provincial banks and townies in general, always seemed to have the proper 'chat up' lines. Nevertheless if a fellow was anyways half good looking and had a hundred acres of land or upwards behind him the astute girl didn't pass him up when asked out to dance. The fellow with bad breath was given a wide berth. When the band struck up and he headed for the line of wallflowers there was a hasty exit to the 'Ladies'. The desire to spend a penny over ruled the desire to dance!

Speaking of music, there was no shortage of small two-piece

or three-piece bands, usually made up of accordion and drums, piano and drums, and maybe a sax player thrown in for good measure. The popular one round our parish was 'Jim Dunny and his Band'. Jimmy and brother Pat were a hard act to follow. Jimmy played piano and accordion, Pat played drums. A fellow called Rodgers sometimes ably assisted them, I can't remember his first name, on sax. If Jimmy wasn't available a fellow called John Grogan took his place. His nickname was 'Fingers' for obvious reasons. They were all brilliant musicians; 'Fingers' Grogan on piano would make you get up in the middle of the night to dance. Jimmy had another attribute that made him so popular. Acting as M C he had everyone in the hall under his eye and if he spotted a situation developing between boy and girl he made the most of it. "The next dance will be a slow fox trot and it's a special request by"—he would mention some girl of boys name, "for so and so". This drew laughter from the crowd and blushes from the girl mentioned, and the lad would get similar treatment from those around him. A Xmas dance with mistletoe hanging from the ceiling he'd really go to town. Stopping the music when he got the right couple under it he'd refuse to play on until everyone was satisfied that the girl had been kissed properly! There were 'excuse me' dances, mixed 'excuse me' dances, 'ladies choice', and the inevitable 'Paul Jones', men on the outside ladies on the inside and circle. Slowing down and speeding up as you circled, hoping to stop opposite the man or girl of your desires! Looking back on those days, compared to today, it was harmless and simple fun. Now we read in our newspapers of young folk falling out of late night drinking dens and puking on the streets, or being carted off to hospitals injured and dead drunk. Perhaps the old Protestant ethic of behaving oneself in public had a point!

Attending Sunday school was another feature of my tender years. In our parish it was always held after morning service (Matins): attendance was mandatory, (no escape). The holding of it after morning service had a rational, that is if you were a 'grown up'. Children travelled with their parents to church by car, rare enough, by bicycle, riding on the crossbar if you were small, pony and trap, and 'shanks mare' (walking). Church attendance had a social as well as spiritual dimension; it gave people the chance to meet up and catch up on things happening, not only in the locality but also far a field. No TV, and radios were scarce enough, to keep people informed and up to scratch! In essence, parents didn't mind hanging around waiting for their kids being fed more spiritual food, blandly ignoring the fact that they the kids already had had a full hour of it! It's easy while away the time yarning about the price of stock, the crops, the state of the nation in general, and first, last, and all the time the weather.

Sunday school at best, could be described as light relief, at worst, an extension of the hour one had just sat through with little comprehension of what it was all about. I've always suspected that if adults were honest they too probably suffered some lack of comprehension, but those times were 'God fearing times', and to turn up and show reverence was sufficient to keeping on side. At least in Sunday school there was no possibility of a dig in the ribs from an over zealous parent if one got a bit fidgety from sitting too long.

Our Sunday school was small in numbers, nevertheless it boasted a senior and a junior class, and consequently we had two teachers. They were sisters, one married, one single, and neither chick not child between them. Tall and angular they towered over us kids; they must have appeared Amazonian in our eyes.

They were also the last line of Ascendancy stock and dressed accordingly. Long tweed jackets over long tweed skirts almost to the ankles, underneath, heavy wool stockings or socks. We kids would never know which type they were, and I don't think we were all that anxious to find out! Large hats clamped on their heads added to their overall height. This whole ensemble gave them a formidable and autocratic appearance. However looks can be deceptive, underneath their stern exteriors were a kindly pair of women. Maybe the fact that they had no children of their own had them a bit at sea as to how to manage children, or maybe they wanted to act as surrogate mothers for the brief half hour in the week that was allotted to them. Whatever the reasons, we kids cottoned on and played on their weaknesses.

Speaking from memory the teaching format was simple enough. Juniors sat in the very last pew and the spinster faced them from the next pew. Seniors sat one up from her and were taken by the married lady. A chapter was read to us, usually from the New Testament, I suppose they didn't want us asking about all the begetting that went on in the Old Testament, especially the spinster woman! Then we were given the verse, with the punch line to learn off by heart for the following week. If next week we could rhyme it off, we got a stamp that was duly fixed into a stamp book A small prize was given at a later date, probably at Xmas. The whole session could have been over in less than ten minutes, but we dragged it out asking inane and awkward questions and if someone didn't know their verse by heart on the following week a million and one excuses were offered up. The end result? All got stamps; consequently all got a small prize! If ever two women deserved heaven it was that pair!

There was another lady in our parish with strong fundamentalist religious thinking, who must have considered us kids heathens of a high order; she set up a second Sunday school to save us all from Hell and Damnation. The lady in question originally came from the North and if my memory serves me right was a Methodist, but as there was no Methodist community in the area she hooked up with the Baptists. Like the other pair, although married, she was childless, but I don't think she had any desire to be a surrogate mother: to save souls and get the Word across was her ambition. This she did fervently. Coming from the North where they take life more serious than the laser-faire attitude of Southerners, she fought an uphill battle with us little heathens!

With Sundays already annexed, she decided to go mid-week, mid afternoon. It was a clever ploy on her part for she lived within a stone's throw of the local Protestant school, thus ensuring a continuity of supply as we headed homewards after the stroke of three. Contrary to what people might think we kids took to the idea like ducks to water. As most of us were farm kids, to go straight home was to be faced with farm chores of some sort, if only gathering twigs for fire starting. This new venture had an element of excitement about it! For starters it was different, tho' the concept was the same; to instil a modicum of reverence and spirituality into our irreverent souls. This was to be achieved by plenty of hymn singing, hand clapping, and a general joie-de- vivre approach. The down side to this new approach as far as we, the backsliders, were concerned, was there were no stamp books, consequently no prizes, but we did get tea and biscuits. Even the approach of our new teacher to the job of saving souls was different; in a word it was militant! As far as she was concerned time was of the essence if we were to be snatched from the jaws of Hell. As far as we were concerned, this singing, hand clapping, and stepping around like the Grand

Old Duke of York was great craic. The tunes, if not the words of the hymns we sang, are indelibly printed in my mind to this very day. For one of them we had to form a circle the opening lines started so; "Jesus bids us shine like a clean pure light"—, and each verse ended with the words, "You in your small corner and I in mine." At the end of each verse to emphasize our corners we had to point at one another. This brought about great swinging of arms and jabbing of fingers causing mirth and mayhem in equal proportions. No one was left out! The starting lines of another one were—"I am H-A-P-P-Y, I am H-A-P-P-Y, I know I am, I'm sure I am, I am H-A-P-P-Y." Those who took the whole session seriously rendered this in doleful fashion, and in manic fashion by those who wanted to let it all hang out! Today I often wonder if we and other groups like us were the forerunners of today's Pop Groups! With teacher belting it out on the piano we gave it our all.

Keeping law and order was a constant challenge for teacher and when at the piano she was at a considerable disadvantage, for her back was to us as we stood in semi-circle around her, girls on the inner circle boys on the outer. For those who wanted to be disruptive it was the ideal situation. I can't say for sure if the lusty singing produced lust of another kind even at that tender age, but the girls in front got their share of attention in the form of hair pulling, poking, and general teasing. Two in particular got more than their share. One wore a long pleat of hair down the middle of her back and got repeated tugging. A shake of the head resettled the plat and a withering look was meant to settle the cough of the culprit. All to know avail. The other girl wore her hair long and loose to her shoulders and with sultry looks to match got plenty of attention!

At this stage of my life I can't say one way or another if this evangelical happy - clappy way to Heaven was, or is the Way, but it did have one lasting effect; it produced singers. All down the years and to this very day my Roman Catholic friends repeatedly say to me,—"All you Protestants are bloody great singers".

My sister and I started our learning years attending Carnalway National School, passing through the local village Brannockstown, about a mile distant from home, to get there. Our first mode of transport was a pony and trap sedately trotting through the village every school day, twice a day. Then a quantum leap was taken; the school bus arrived. Not your modern day 50 or 30 seater, but in the form of a Model T Ford post van, with planking either side for seats. Those first picked up had a choice of seats, the last ones, sister and me squatted on the floor. The bus wore the national colour and the post logo. It was driven by a tubby genial sort of man called Barber, who wore very thick glasses and had a modern day skinhead haircut. He was practically bald! A jack of all trades, today's entrepreneur, he lived in Killcullen dealing in scrap engine parts, attending to the town's waterworks system, and delivering the mail from Killcullen the main post office then, to surrounding offices in the area. The post van, probably the only van in the area was the obvious choice to do the school run. For the life of me I can't remember his first name but he would have been Mister to us kids anyway. Respect for your elders ruled in those times! Travelling with him at all times was a security man, a son called Jimmy probably aged about thirteen or fourteen. Jimmy controlled the sophisticated and elaborate mechanism that opened and closed the back doors, yet it was simplicity itself, keeping us kids from falling out. Two large staples were driven into both doors. A length of string was fastened onto one staple then run through the other one and pulled tight by Jimmy. Pull, doors were shut, loosen off, doors open! A masterpiece in design and operation and insurance proof of course.

I clearly remember two episodes from those bus runs. The first one concerned a family of three, a brother and two sisters. Wild as mountain goats they were and into every devilment that was going. I should explain that the bus stopped at "Tims" or "O'Briens Corner", it went by either name, to pick up the sister and myself. We were the last on the run. "Tims" to give it its proper name was a shop run by Timothy M Doyle who had rented space (the parlour) from O'Briens to run his business. A typical country shop of the times he sold everything from a needle to not quite the anchor. On the evening run the pressure was obviously off 'Ol man Barber for he always stopped at "Tims" and went in to buy cigarettes and yarn with Tim or anyone else in there. This was the golden opportunity for two of the Three Musketeers to go into action. Out would hop the brother and head for the starting handle. No electronic ignition in those days, no switch key; a magneto supplied the spark which duly arrived to the spark plugs when the engine was cranked. One of the sisters got into the drivers seat to manipulate the two levers under the steering wheel; a hand throttle was one, the other controlled the spark from the magneto. A quick pull on the starting handle and the engine would burst into life. Sister would yank the hand throttle wide open, the engine would scream its head off, and Ol man Barber would come dashing out of the shop breathing fire and brimstone. Brother would duck behind the van; sister would tumble over the driver's seat, her skirt above her hips displaying vivid green drawers. This action and display drew howls of laughter from the spectators. This stunt was pulled many times, and apart from threats and dire warnings, I never once saw Ol man Barber raise a hand to either of the pair. A variation on the theme was for sister to pull a fast one on brother. She would retard the magneto lever thus causing the engine to backfire. The starting crank would kick back against brother's arm causing him to do a jig of pain as he nursed a sore wrist, the engine would splutter, then Bang, a mighty shot came out of the exhaust. The crows roosting in the Harristown oaks opposite the shop would lift off, cawing and flapping, then fly out of the war zone to the beech trees overlooking the River Liffey half a mile away. Ol man Barber came running.

The second story concerns Billy, Ol man Barber's eldest son, and George Cardiff's rooster. Billy must have been a man of means for he drove a high powered open tourer Sunbeam. When father got snowed under with work Billy stepped in and did the school run, much to our delight, for if the day was fine we travelled in style with the hood down waving to all and sundry. Being young and exuberant Billy had one speed—flat out, in all gears. Making his last 'pick up' at Tim's one fine summer morning, Billy gunned the motor. Flat out in second he rounded the first bend in the village spewing gravel over the low wall into Jamsie Gagan's garden and slipped her into third. Approaching George Cardiff's at a rate of knots he found fourth and slammed his throttle foot to the floor.

George Cardiff was also a man of means. The area postman, (up hill and down dale in all weathers on a bicycle) he was also a land owner. His house was behind a high wall on one side of the village, his land and farm buildings on the other side. About twelve acres in all, enough to keep a cow, a few weanlings, a scatter of hens, and a prize rooster. On this fateful morning the rooster was preening himself on top of the high wall. Maybe he was planning a visit to his harem on the far side, or feeling depressed and planning suicide, I'll never know, but he made his move just as the Sunbeam bore down on him. Like a Boeing 747 he launched himself off the wall, wings at full stretch. Suddenly he lost altitude and was caught by the Sunbeam's windscreen —Wham. The wind force lifted him off the windscreen and dumped him amongst us in the back seat, a tangled gory mess of blood, feathers, and crushed flesh. Were we little savages distressed or dismayed? Not one iota. Shrieks of laughter, and those who had managed to avoid being splattered with blood and guts soon had it daubed on them so that we were all look-a-likes. If this slaughter on the roads upset Billy he didn't show it, just drove on like a man possessed, reaching over the windshield to remove a tail feather that had got caught under the wiper. On arriving at school splattered with blood and pieces of feathers stuck to us, the look on the teachers face indicated that we were an advance party of Indian Braves on the warpath.

The whole episode kept us in conversation for the day, each telling those not fortunate enough to have witnessed the macabre scene, as to how it was, and keeping us all from the boredom of class. It may be a sad reflection on my life and evidence of wasted years that my memory fails to recall anything more exciting than these two stories during those formative years! However, I did learn one thing. Kids, are sadistic little buggers.

Chapter 3
The Hungry Thirties

We as a family would have been described as middle class farmers sitting on something over two hundred acres. A large farm by Irish standards, but put into perspective not as large as some of our neighbours. On our west side was, and still is, a large estate of one thousand acres. Others nearby are approximately four hundred. Squeezed in between are Land Commissioned holdings of twenty two acres, (poverty traps). The whole area could be described as grazing lands, with a moderate amount under the plough, unlike south Kildare noted for its tillage output. It was and is 'Big House' and 'horse country'. The houses have stayed the occupants changed! Some of the lands are now owned by foreign nationals and to their credit are kept in immaculate condition. In a sense little has changed in this immediate area over the years. Stud and dairy farms mix in with sheep and cattle grazing, and everyone aspires to owning a horse! Predominately it is still a grazing area.

Our own situation in the Thirties, and those around us, was much the same all over Ireland; farmers hadn't a tosser (money). But the old saying, if you haven't got it you won't miss it, applied. Waste was not a topic of conversation amongst rural folk, for the simple reason, like the money we didn't have it, and what we had we made use of. Household waste, (food) took a trip to the farmyard where eager mouths awaited it, usually a pig or pigs. Calves slurped skim milk; small potatoes were boiled, mashed up with oats, and fed to hens, ducks, and turkeys. Domestic pets, cats and dogs hoovered up tit bits. If there was anything left over after that lot was seen to, it went into the farmyard manure heap where it returned to the land as rotted compost. Year in year out, perpetual motion personified. Today, that champion of soil fertility, farmyard manure, is under suspicion as a polluter of our waters!

In this modern world of high technology it seems ironic that local authorities and governments of the day seem to spend an inordinate amount time discussing 'waste', and what to do about it. Consumer waste, factory waste, pit waste, daily papers radio programs and TV discussions, carry stories about what to do, or what not to do about these mountains of waste that are piling up 'No Dump Here', or 'No Incinerator Wanted' signs, are frequently seen as one drives through the countryside.

In the times I speak of, waste or waste management, wouldn't have raised a discussion at a crossroads let alone on a radio or TV program. Not from a rural perspective anyway. In the 'Hungry Thirties' that old dictum 'waste not, want not, was the motto of all who strove to make a living from the land. What could be saved was saved, and not only saved but recycled, and recycled a second time if at all possible. And that motto applied to all those who lived in a rural area. An immediate example comes to mind. If a loaf of bread was purchased in the local village shop it was most likely to be wrapped in a sheet of yesterday's unsold daily paper. When the loaf arrived in the farm kitchen, it's wrapping was carefully put aside and used later on to wrap eggs in, to be sold in the village shop, thus returning the paper to it's place of origin. A large roll of new brown wrapping paper hung on a roller with a cutting edge, but was only used when the shopkeeper ran out of 'dailys'. Waste not, want not, was set deep in the rural Irish psyche. Today, a health inspector would probably slap a 'closed' sign on the shop, on the grounds that all that paper movement was spreading some mysterious disease.

The Hungry Thirties were not peculiar to Ireland, for depression ranged world over. In the States and Canada it was called the Dusty Thirties due to years of drought, and dust storms blew across the prairies smothering struggling grain crops causing endless hardship there. Europe had high unemployment, which brought troubles of a different kind eventually sparking off World War 2. We had a special name for our unique position. It was called, The Economic War! Dev (De Valara) was the leader of the government of the day. In his wisdom, (farmers would say stupidity), he reneged on an agreement with the British Government that was made at the formation of the Irish State. I don't know the exact arrangements, but apparently he refused to reimburse the British with monies due, in exchange for loss of land rents, or annuities as they were called. Naturally, the British Government took a dim view of this, and slapped an embargo on all Irish imports into England. It was a disastrous decision for Ireland. At the time she had little enough exports, and what they were, were mainly agricultural, cattle, fat and store, being the big ones. Not only that, but England was about the only country we exported to. Prices flopped, animals became unsaleable, and agriculture went into a tailspin.

However, like all sanctions or embargoes, ways and means were concocted to circumvent the rules. There was another factor that was a help. England was an industrial country and needed imports of food to feed the nation. Food came into England from far afield; Argentina shipped large amounts of beef, but Ireland was nearer and could supply fresh beef, not frozen. Shipped over live on the hoof they were much sought after by English butchers. It was an advantage not to be missed! The British government had to look over both shoulders at one and the same time, a not insurmountable manoeuvre for any government, either then or now. Those uppity Irish had to be slapped down, but food, especially fresh food, kept voters happy, and so a system of 'quotas' was introduced. I suppose one could call them; an English solution to an Irish - English problem! The quota system went something like this. England allowed a percentage of fat cattle to be imported into England, but the distribution, or put another way; the handing out of permits was implemented by the Irish Department of Agriculture. In no time flat a thriving black market in permits was under way. Anyone 'well got' with a certain political party didn't appear to have much trouble in shifting a few 'fats' and a few for 'well got' neighbours also. Anyone operating along the Border was in clover. Irish cattle became English cattle with one skip and jump! A big time shipper of cattle with a home base near Dundalk was often seen at fairs handing out permits like snuff at a wake. The back hander (commission) earned on these permits would more than fill the petrol tank of the big car he drove.

As a small gossoon most of this 'carry on' was over my head, nevertheless, snippets of conversation and gossip were there for the listening for any small boy with sharp ears. And there was lots of it. At every church gate, crossroads, over the hedge between neighbours, and at the focal point of Irish agricultural business, — the Fair Day, permits were the main topic of conversation. A typhoon, earthquake, or any such world catastrophe would come a poor second as a topic of conversation anywhere a group of farmers gathered to 'shoot the breeze'. A conversation would go something like this.

"Any luck Bill?"

"Yea, I'm gettin' a few shifted next week" The exact number was top secret!

"Good be God,—I hear yer man is gettin' some away too" This innocent remark is half question seeking confirmation.

"Sure why wouldn't he, ya know the way he votes. Didn't he get some away the week afore last." It was always assumed that anyone who seemed to be getting more than their share of quota was voting 'the right way', or knew what doors to knock on!

"Any luck yerself?"

"Keepin' the fingers crossed. A lad was supposed to drop in a few permits ere yesterday but no sign of any yet. I'm in no hurry anyroads, sure the price is shite." This last remark was one of defiance, as if he didn't care if he never got a permit, and all shysters, chancers, and permit swappers could go an' be damned as far as he was concerned. A bit of bravado wouldn't prevent him from accepting the permits when they did arrive, backdoor or otherwise. This whole 'quota' business was all hush hush. An aura of secrecy hung over any conversation. Names were never mentioned, and individuals were referred to as—Yer man, yer wan, the boyo, the bucko. These code or trade names would have sounded confusing to an outsider, but the insider (cattlemen) knew exactly who was being referred to. Where these folk lived was also under code. He lived, be'yant, down the road, over the way, or, out along such an such road. In this day and age the whole 'quota system' and how it worked, would qualify to be put in a classified information file!

So much for aids to agriculture; at the other end of the spectrum were the poor, and there were plenty of them around both in city and countryside. The modern welfare state hadn't yet been invented, nevertheless the government did recognise that there was poverty in the land, especially amongst the working classes, and so they set up a scheme to help fill empty bellies. I don't remember the official title, but in the countryside it was called 'The Free Beef', and became the butt of much jocular and ribald comment. If some feat of strength was accomplished it was put down to the 'free beef', or if another baby appeared in an already large family in a labourer's cottage, it was put down to the 'free beef'! Like all well intentioned government schemes either then or now this one had its fault lines, and it didn't take long for anyone with an eye to making a few bob (money) to see the possibilities. Rules and regulations are always set up to run government schemes, especially free ones; implementing them is the difficult bit. One man in the parish dropped a lucrative trade and became a butcher literally overnight. He set up a slaughterhouse and butchers block in an old farm building, and in no time flat was giving out 'free beef'. Stripper cows (cows whose useful life is at an end) were bought for next to nothing and converted into real money, government backed! It was money for old rope. He expanded the business, bought a Ford truck, and put a man on the road selling meat door to door. The truck would come barrelling down our avenue (quarter mile) raising clouds of dust in summer, a green tarpaulin meant to cover the meat flapping in the breeze. Arriving at the hall door the driver would pull back the tarpaulin and expose lengths and sides of beef. While the housewife, in this case my mother, made pleasant conversation with the driver, flies buzzed and settled on the exposed sides of meat. A choice was made, cash changed hands, and if it wasn't available on the spot sure it was OK till next time he called. If per chance a housewife chose a piece of stripper cow instead of prime beef, well that was her choosing, and no one knew the difference only her self and the husband when they sat down to eat it. By then it was too late! And if per chance a meat inspector came peddling up the avenue on his bike (unlikely event) to break up the pleasant conversation, what ever about passing comment on the host of flies, his knowledge of stripper cow and prime steak in the raw was negligible

This butcher man went on to greater things. He had that inordinate ability to spot a project that had money written all over it. When war broke out he saw a need for fuel wood and went into the timber business. He bought up trees, had them felled, sawn up, and split, then delivered the logs to the fuel dump in the Phoenix Park, which was used to keep Dublin people warm. When the war was over he went into the building business, which had stagnated during the war, then took off when hostilities ceased. He died a very wealthy man, and never set a foot out of Ireland! Begrudgers, take note.

Money, in scarce supply in those times was certainly not wasted, and in some cases a form of barter replaced the necessity for it. Neighbours sharing their labour at haymaking and thrashings were a prime example. At these gatherings, with the work done and bellies filled with soda bread liberally coated with jam, and all washed down with strong tay, it was time for swapping gossip and news, and sometimes a bit of extra diversion thrown in.

A local widow woman on a tidy bit of land had the neighbours in giving a hand at saving the hay. It was known as a 'good house,' meaning, that the grub would not only be well cooked, but there'd be lashings of it. The group contained a couple of pranksters, and their eyes fell on a horse's cart parked in the haggard where the work was taking place. Nearby was an outhouse, part of the small but well kept farmyard. The door of the outhouse was a conventional one permitting entrance or exit for one individual. With nothing on their minds but devilment the two jokers proceeded to take the wheels off the cart; then with a bit of help from the onlookers they carried the cart into the outhouse replacing the wheels once inside. It was never related as to how the widda got the cart out again, but I'm sure there was all hell to pay!

Pitching hay or stooking sheaves was hot dusty work and the arrival of tay in the field at around four o'clock was always welcome. Men stuck their forks into the ground and headed to the spot where mugs were being filled and sandwiches laid out. If there were a big number to be fed, the tay was carried in an enamel bucket covered with a cloth; the sandwiches in a large wicker basket. This chore was usually carried out by the housewife, daughter, or maybe a slip of a girl working as a maid. Sometimes all three, or a combination of the three, for the women also enjoyed the opportunity to get a break from house work, a chance to get a breath of fresh air and maybe get a bit of gossip besides. And if per chance the maid got a sly wink from one of the lads, sure that was a bonus!

Stories abound about such events. On one occasion there was a sandwich left over. It was passed around the group each one politely refusing, leaving it to the other fellow. Eventually an arm stretched out to accept the last offering with the comment.

"Jasus lads, don't send anythin' back, there could less come out tomorrow." This piece of philosophy coming from the rural savant contained an element of truth on two fronts. He was the father of a large family and found it difficult to keep food on the table at times. To send a sandwich back where it might be thrown to the dog was anathema to his way of thinking. Secondly, the farmer's wife who had produced it, if not exactly mean, was known to run a tight house budget, and would probably take note of the lone returning sandwich!

Neighbourly help was not solely confined to the harvest or hay field. One Sunday morning three stout men having got Mass, were returning homewards dressed in their Sunday best. They were walking. It was early springtime and the fields had taken on a green hue brought about by the first sprouting of grass shoots. On the open fields they were scarce enough, but down in the gripes where there was shelter there was enough to tempt a hungry animal who had come through the lean times of winter. Suddenly, the journey of the three lads was halted by cries of help coming from a neighbour in an adjoining field. One of his cows had yielded to temptation. Reaching for a fresh bite she had taken a step too far and had slid down into the gripe. She was stuck fast.

On any occasion such as this, the first thing to do is to take an overall look and appraise the job at hand. There is also a diversity of opinions as to the best way to handle the situation!

"Be gor a macky she's well held," is the first observation.

"Cripes, she is at that," confirms the first opinion.

"Jakers, ye may go for a horse an' rope," is the first concrete suggestion as to how the job should be tackled.

"Hould yer hoult ther a minute, sure maybee a bit iva lift be the tail might shift her."

This opinion offers a second option, and comes from one of the 'hard' men anxious to show his strength. On this occasion a compromise was arrived at. They'd first give her 'a bit iva lift be the tail' and should that fail the horse and rope would be called upon.

Anxious to show their muscle the three stalwarts slid down into the gripe and grabbed the cow by the tail. With an encouraging shout of --"Now lads, heave," they heaved. In a jiffy the cow's tail end was pointing skywards. With head down and tail up the animal was probably in discomfort and under stress. It should be mentioned that fresh spring grass loosens the bowels of all animals. This cow was no exception. She coughed. From her rear end shot a stream of green smelly scutter catching the three full frontal. Prayers of a kind different to the ones they had uttered less than an hour previous fell from their lips. Cursing, swearing, and pulling wads of old dried grass and leaves to try and wipe the worst of it off, the three climbed out of the gripe. To add insult to injury the cow scrambled to her feet continued down the ditch aways and finding a spot where the bank was broken climbed up and proceeded to graze as if nothing had happened. This event kept the parish in chat for manys the long day.

The shortage of money didn't prevent rural people from getting along with their lives. I've already mentioned the barter system, and the willingness of people to help each other free of charge. Self sufficiency was a big asset. All farms and cottage gardens produced food for the table. A pig was fattened for home consumption and a lot of meat was got off the carcass of a two year old wether (castrated sheep). On farms where labour was employed the worker got free milk and firewood, and a drill or two of spuds (potatoes) depending on the length of drill.

Most people knew how to set a snare, so rabbit meat was also a staple. Ironically, in spite of the many streams and rivers in Ireland one seldom heard of fresh fish being on the menu in rural households. 'Fish of a Friday' was mandatory at the time in Catholic Ireland, but the fish came from the sea and were purchased either at a local shop, or from a travelling van man who travelled from door to door selling everything from a needle to an anchor, --well almost everything! In a general statement one could say that all farms retained what was necessary for both human and animal welfare, and after that any surplus was sold. The cash generated from the surplus went back into the farm. If a choice had to be made between a new collar for the horse, or a new dress for the wife, the horse usually won out!

The rural poverty line, if one could define it as such, could be drawn between the small farm and upwards and the working classes. The 'Labouring Man' and his wife had very little of life's luxuries. Manys the man turned up for work in the morning on an empty stomach, and for lunch had the luxury of eating a couple of slices of bread with drippin'(lard) spread between them. His clothes very often were 'hand me downs' the cast off's of the farmer he was working for, likewise his foot ware. It was a help if he and his employer were of like build, otherwise some needle work by the wife was required. Boots were soled and re-soled, and if leather wasn't to hand an old car tire came in handy. Cut in strips it out wore leather. Stitching or tacking it to well worn uppers was an art form! Hob nail boots were standard wear. Tough unyielding leather in the uppers, the soles were half an inch thick with two rows of nails around the outside and three rows down the centre. Provided the nails were replaced as they wore the soles remained good. In fact the boots were almost indestructible and almost impossible to wear for after many wettings and then drying out they became as hard as the hob a Hell. Wellington or rubber boots were not popular, and not easily available. It was said at the time—"that they were bad for the feet"!

Piped water was unheard of, let alone bathrooms or toilets, and that applied to some of the farmhouses as well. Water from the roof was collected in a barrel placed under a down pipe, which was connected to the gutters. This water was used for ordinary washing purposes. Water for drinking and cooking was drawn from a spring well. Sanitary needs were taken care of by the 'pot under the bed'. That took care of nocturnal urges; the daytime ones had a choice in the wide-open spaces! Fellows standing at a crossroads near home playing the last game of 'pitch and toss' or just plain gossiping, would break up and retire for the night when they saw Bridie Murphy going out to the haggard to relieve herself. "Time for bed lads, Bridie has made her water," would be the comment. With the Angelus ringing out at noon and six, and Bridie's last performance at around ten, these were the timepieces that rural folk set their own watches by. But there was no great urgency about time either, "Come day go day and God send Sunday" was an oft repeated phrase.

The middle class or 'stout farmer' and his family were into more sophisticated arrangements; they had the luxury of the outdoor toilet. Great effort and thought went into the design and placement of this edifice. It had to be unobtrusive and yet readily accessible. Not too far from the dwelling house nor yet too near, and account was taken of which way the prevailing wind blew! Beside, or on, a gravel pathway was desirous; no point in having to traipse through wet grass to get there. The ideal location was somewhere in the garden, possibly behind the apple trees, or built into or behind a high hedge. To be discreetly positioned relative to the dwelling was the objective. The structure itself was modest enough inside. A wooden seat or bench with the appropriate hole ran along the back wall. Down in the void under the hole was a bucket to catch the 'waste'. The distance between bucket and hole was carefully calculated. Too near, and you got splash; too far, and you ran the risk of a 'miss'. On the bench for your convenience was a pile of papers, usually old newspapers (recycling at its best) or some such material, softer if possible. A more sophisticated arrangement was a nail driven into the woodwork and squares of paper (12 x 12) neatly hanging from the nail. There was a social order for the usage of the building. The farm owner and his nearest and dearest, visitors, a servant girl, or the woman who came in once a week to help on 'wash days'. The bucket was emptied on a regular basis, usually by the lowest member of the work force. I once saw one built over a stream. To day, it would have a prohibition order placed on it! These 'outhouses' were probably the forerunner of to days Port-a-loo.

The shortage of money didn't prevent people from enjoying themselves. Entertainment in some respects cost little. Visiting each other's houses just for a gossip, or maybe play a hand of cards, 25's was the popular game. Visiting from house to house was called mitchin' and some houses were more popular than others. Very often if there was a musician in the gathering a bit of a dance got goin'. With or without music these gatherings ran late into the night. A sod of turf or stick would be thrown on dying embers and as the fire picked up so did the conversation, another mug of strong tay would be passed round. The local cinema, or picture house as it was called was another form of entertainment. An old shilling (5pence) got you a good seat, 2/ shillings luxury class. There you could see Tom Mix, Gene

Autry, Spencer Tracy, Gabby Hayes, Rita Hayworth, the stars of Hollywood almost in your lap. Summer evenings at any crossroads would be a crowd playing pitch an' toss. A gambling game played with pennies. The only thing at a crossroads nowadays is a Stop or Yield sign. Ferreting rabbits, another pass time that had the advantage of putting meat on the table, and if you had a good day's ferreting there was always sale for any surplus. The odd house had a wireless set (radio) run on batteries, and when there was a football or hurling final being played that place was a full house! If the day was fine all sat outside and listened. The discussion that took place after the match often lasted longer than the match itself, and the only thing that broke it up was cows waiting to be milked!

Chapter 4
Hitler's War

Hitler was the first man to put a bit of jiz and money into Irish agriculture by starting a war! I think it was Napoleon who coined the phrase that 'an army marches on its belly' and how true. Suddenly there was a demand for food from across the water. The book on 'beef quotas' was quietly closed, and anything we could produce was acceptable. Not just beef, but everything that was edible. The 'Economic War' of the 'Hungry Thirties' disappeared into the shadows as World War 2 of the 'Forties came into view, with the Allies squaring up to Hitler. A new 'directive' from the Department of Agriculture was issued. All farmers had to plough; I think it was 15%, of their arable land, and a host of inspectors criss-crossed the country to ensure the directive was adhered to. It was hardly necessary, for farmers don't look a gift horse in the mouth. It was probably their first opportunity to earn some decent money since Independence. The crop yield wasn't as good as to-days, for artificial fertilisers were practically non-existent. For a good return from wheat an old lea sod was the ideal or a field that had roots in it the previous year. Rotation was sound farming practice.

The 'down side' to the war as far as Ireland was concerned was rationing of imports, and believe it or not some of those imports were foodstuffs,—tea and sugar, two commodities much loved by all, to mention just two. But practically all foodstuffs were rationed in an effort to supply the 'war effort'. Fuel oil for tractors was rationed and private cars were off the road, not that there were many of them around, but tractors were beginning to appear on big farms. Just like the 'beef quotas' in the Thirties a thriving black market was soon flourishing in all commodities that were rationed. Anyone with money, or in the 'know', could always get that little bit extra. The word Spiv became part of the English language! Ditties to commemorate rationing flowed freely. One comes to mind.

Will ye come to the weddin' will ye come
Bring your own tay and sugar an' a bun.

On the whole, one could say that Ireland had a good war when compared to the rest of Europe in terms of hardship, and folk living in rural parts were better off than those confined to towns and cities. The 'cabbage garden' was still cultivated. There was work for all, tho' most of it was across the water, building airstrips, working in munitions factories, contributing to the war effort, and able to send a few quid (pounds) home!

With the war over and the Fifties approaching the world in general set to with a will. There was lots to be done. There was a scarcity of everything except perhaps guns and bombs, and they were no longer needed. But everything else such as building and development had been put on hold, now it was all systems go. The Colonies, as they were then known, Australia, New Zealand, Canada, and large tracts of Africa were open to all comers. Back in war torn Europe, cities had to be rebuilt and motorways laid. No green cards or working permits necessary; your ability to work was your passport to a better life. Paddy, along with thousands of displaced persons from Eastern Europe answered the call. Not since the Famine was there such an exodus from Ireland. Working for the 'war effort' had shown Paddy a different way of life, and more important, had put money in his pocket. Now, here was the chance to improve. This exodus had a detrimental effect on Ireland. I well remember the comment of a neighbour who had experience of hard times pre World War 2, when even then emigration was the only chance to better oneself He was referring to 'election promises' made, when land and money was promised to all, and how Ireland was well free of English rule. "With the election won the promises were quietly forgotten, and we all went off to work for the 'inemy' (England)," was his wry comment!

Her three green fields remained green, and stagnant. The fourth one benefited from England's coffers. This was most evident concerning agriculture. England's post war government was determined that her farmers should be kept commercially viable and introduced subsidies. A day trip across the Border was a sight for sore eyes from an agricultural point of view. Well kept hedges and buildings, machinery up to date; the farms smelt of money. South of the Border we were almost back in the Thirties. A wall of protectionism was built around what industries we had, and State backed industries gobbled up money like there was no tomorrow. They did however give employment. It was said at the time that it was an expensive form of dole.

The birth of the Land Drainage Scheme and a subsidy on ground limestone in the mid Fifties, was the first recognition by the government of the day that farmers made up part of the population. Generous grants for drainage and the sub on ground limestone kick-started agriculture back into life. But the biggest kick came from the farmers themselves. Realising that muscle was needed, not only on the land, but also in their dealings with respective governments, branches of the IFA (Irish Farmers Association) then known as the NFA, were set up around the country. Governments sat up and took notice! Coupled with the ICMSA (Irish Creamery Milk Suppliers Association) these two formidable organisations have gone from strength to strength and have considerable clout not only at government level but in Europe as well. But in spite of tough negotiations and farmer's marches, farming has remained second citizen to industry. Throughout the remainder of the Fifties and into the Sixties the urban rural split possible widened.

In the Sixties, a man with vision and bright ideas working in the Department of Finance (an unusual spot for either) laid his thoughts before the Leader of the Day and had them accepted, thus starting off Ireland's Industrial Revolution! Farming remained on the sidelines. The man who had the bright ideas was T K Whittaker. The man who took the gamble was Sean Lemass. At the same time there were rumours and counter rumours about Ireland joining the EEC as it was called then. Farmers sat and waited for confirmation. England was still our best customer for our farm produce but she didn't pay over the odds! There were millions of mouths to be filled in Europe and farmers couldn't wait to cast their vote.

Chapter 5
War and Horses

It was World War 2 I suppose that kept us in the horse age longer than necessary for cars were off the road except for essential services (doctors, clergy, etc) and fuel for tractors on the land was rationed. The working draft was still king and on most farms was aided and abetted by a working cob, a tidy animal that could pull a spring dray (small cart with springs) scuffle turnip or mangel drills, and take the family to worship on Sundays in a pony trap or to shop, or pay a yearly visit to relatives who lived in distant parts. Distant parts being a range of twenty to twenty five miles away. A good cob was also good for a days hunting.

But if the advent of the war kept us backward agriculturally speaking, it brought about a lively trade in practically all classes of horses, especially the cob or good hunter and the turnover was quick. Like training your own sheepdog some farmers liked breaking their own horses, but most of them had neither the time nor inclination to do so. This is where the specialist stepped in, and Father considered himself a specialist in horse matters. He moved swiftly to fill a gap in the market. No matter where or what the demand was, he was prepared to fill it. Racers, working animals, hunters, to him they were all just horses, and he could handle each and every situation. What the customer wants the customer gets, you could say was his motto.

As previously mentioned he had spent his early years in the "Wild West" of Canada breaking wild horses. The breaking methods used there, as compared to here, were as different as chalk is from cheese. Three or four men would somehow or other get a rope 'round the animals neck, snub the rope to a post, and let him run 'round it till he ran out of rope. Now under control of sorts a blanket or jacket would be thrown over his head, and then grabbed by an ear and a saddle slapped on his back. The bravest of the bunch would climb aboard and it was all systems go! I think the general idea was to get the message across to the horse that he was no longer foot loose and fancy free roaming the range at will. It was called 'bronco bustin' and we've all read or heard about it. Remarkable enough, with the exception of the odd mean one most horses got the message in double quick time, and the slowest part of the training was teaching him to neck rein (turn left or right). This was done by applying pressure with the reins on the right side of the neck when wanting him to turn left and visa - versa.

Being fortunate to own a reasonably large farm by Irish standards, with three of four men employed, once he got them organised in the morning he could indulge his hobby for the rest of the day which consisted of breaking a young horse, or out in the hunting field in the winter months.

Due to an incidence that took place between him and a customer at a later stage it is worth mentioning that his breaking methods were part bronco bustin', part standard! He didn't believe in wasting time for time was money, so the object was to get the animal moved on and get started on another. But, there's no doubt that the secret of his success was mostly due to the fact that he could very quickly suss out an animal's abilities and work according to those abilities. One shouldn't expect a jackass to win a Derby. He applied the same criteria to his customers and matched them accordingly!

Mind you, a lot of the horses he bought in for breaking were not unlike their Canadian counterparts. Four and five year olds roaming the bottom- lands and bogs of Irish farms, once weaned they were turned out, and neary a hand left on them since that time. Some arrived with burrs sticking to their matted coats, the whites of their eyes rolling in their heads. The first move was to stick a breaking bit in his mouth and leave him chomp on that for a while, then get him on a long rein and ring (lunge) him clockwise and anti-clockwise. Panting and blowing and sufficiently tired a saddle was parked on his back, and then father or a gossunn (self) parked on the saddle. All this took place in a matter of days. Should the animal be heading for a hunting career, he was introduced to a low cut thorn hedge. No fancy painted poles and barrels, for the first tentative jump he'd be faced up to the cut hedge. Should he balk or jib, a dig in the ribs with the spurs and at the same time a cut of the riding crop (stick) on the rump worked wonders. If he fell or pushed through the hedge on first effort, the thinking was that the thorns would tickle his belly and he'd sure jump clear next try! It was rough logic but it worked. Working horses were put through the system at an even faster rate. Once comfortable with bit, collar, hames, and straddle, traces were introduced and the animal was hooked up to pull a length of log or grass-harrow. Ours was the best grass-harrowed farm in the country! Next and last piece of harness to attach was the britchen, and that tailored him to pull a cart. The cob, already mentioned, was in great demand, and was the bread and butter part of the business.

One might ask the question, how come none of these half wild, half broken horses by Irish standards, were never returned as unsuitable? Well, there was a war on with compulsory tillage, farmers were busy and once a horse was purchased he'd be put to work right away not getting any time to reflect on his carefree days. Transition from primary to secondary schooling took place without too many hitches, and if there was one, a few pounds off the original price kept everyone happy and the war effort going! Remember also that Irish people are good with horses and all the purchasers needed were the rough edges taken off, they could do the rest.

Where did he get the raw material, and even more important, how was the marketing of the product accomplished? He roamed the countryside quite a bit himself picking up one or two here and there, but the contact man was the key to continuity of supplies, in both directions. The horse trade in those days were similar to the cattle trade and had its compliment of blockers, dealers, and jobbers, in fact some of them dabbled at the two trades. No mobile phone in their pockets or dangling from their hips, nevertheless they were mines of information, combing and criss-crossing every parish in the area. "Dere's da makin's of a hunter below in Mackie's bog, mebbe ye'd take a look at him yerself if yer passin' sometime." Conversely, "I hear da Colonel is wantin' a hunter for da season" or "da Wida Miley has a good lookin' cob runnin ' on da hill, mebbe ye'ed give her a throw for 'im." The word 'throw' meant an offer of money and had no sexual connotations whatsoever!

Probably the best contact man my Father has was a horse-trading tinker man. Travelling people is the political correct term used today, but in those days they were collectively called tinkers, for the simple reason I suppose was that is exactly what they did. Going 'round the countryside tinkering and fixing things. Repairing and making from new tin cans and kettles, or anything that leaked or needing a bit of fixing, their soldering irons at the ready and all for a few bob or exchange for a meal or the grazing of a pony or horse for the night. This particular man had no 4x4 or shiny aluminium trailer, but a horse drawn caravan of the times, wife and all belongings inside. Maybe some of the clan repaired kettles but not he. He covered the horse fairs of the country and always had something to trade. Father and he had many a deal, hacks, hunters, broken and unbroken, their financial acumen probably on a par with their knowledge of horses. If the wool was going to be pulled over somebody's eyes it wasn't each others. There was one important feature in the role played by this man concerning Fathers operation. As in all businesses there are failures as well as successes, and when too many failures appeared in the back paddock word was got to him, or a visit paid to his camp if near hand. He'd clear the paddock and place them round the country in his own fashion, at discount prices of course. Things haven't changed much, when a commodity passes its sell by date it becomes a liability, especially if it's wolfing down mouthfuls of hay or grass!

And speaking of times past and trades that have disappeared, there was one other travelling family who were once a year visitors to our place. It all happened by chance and there was a horse involved but not for sale or trade. The man and his wife had parked their caravan on a wide verge of roadside just below our entrance gate. Come dark the man put his horse into our field across the road there to rest up for the night and get a belly full of sweet grass. It was standard practice. He'd have him out at daylight and nobody be any the wiser! He didn't reckon on my Father who was always out and about at crack of dawn. Out on his pony at the first streak of daylight Father spotted the horse chomping away to his hearts content. He didn't begrudge the night's keep for the animal; he had thirty acres all to himself, but didn't like being taken for granted. If someone hadn't the grace to ask permission he considered they were trespassing, the number of animals was immaterial. Riding by the caravan where the owner was feeding bits of twigs to a fire in preparation for breakfast he bid the man good morning. "An good morra to yerself Sir," came the reply. "That horse a yours could get a colic from all that fresh grass." There was an element of truth in what he said for it was possible should the animal be given a fast gallop on top of a full belly of food. An unlikely event in the circumstances, but it was a diplomatic way of letting the tinker man know that he'd have to be up a bit earlier in the day should he wish to pull the wool over Fathers eyes! "I'll have him out ere long Boss soon as I get a bit me self, an the blessin's a God on ye an all yourn." Some time later on that day a brand new three quart can was left at the back door. Payment for services rendered one might say! The tinker man hadn't much of this worlds riches but he too had his pride and principles: the gift of the can was his diplomatic way of saying he owed no one. For years afterwards we got a once a year visit from that tinker man and his wife; he would solder a leaking milk or water bucket or sell a new one, my mother would buy clothes pegs from his wife who carried on her hip a large wicker basket filled with pegs, coloured ribbon, and trinkets. These types of people plying their trade and trinkets have long since disappeared off the roads of Ireland. It's impossible to solder a plastic bucket!

Father had one deal that nearly became unstuck. Unfortunately it was with a neighbour who purchased from him a lovely strawberry roan cob, ideally suited to a cob's duties. This animal had a bit of high class blood in him from somewhere, and was a high stepper balanced with a kind temperament. After a tough wrangle a deal was struck and the cob changed hands. A week or two passed and Father noticed the cob turned out on a bit of rough bottom land adjoining our own.

On a late spring early summer's sort of evening Father set off down the road with a fast moving rangy type of hunter, coupled to a high wheeled back to back gig, myself sitting beside him. I usually acted as a sort of insurance or spare part should anything go wrong. He wheeled into the neighbours yard and confronted him, not mincing his words. "I see that cob turned out below, what's the matter." "O God he's gone wild," was the reply. "Wild be damned, get him in here," was the sharp retort. He climbed down from the gig instructing me to take the harness off the hunter and the two headed for the bottom land. Returning with the cob the harness was slapped on him and he was backed into the shafts of the gig. "Get up," was the next command and all climbed aboard, me scrambling into the back.

All gigs carried a carriage whip and Father removed it from its stock as we wheeled out of the yard and turned right up a small hill the cob walking smartly. The other side of the hill was long and steep and on reaching the top Father cracked the whip right over the cob's ears. The animal exploded. In jet like fashion he tore down that hill scattering stones left, right, and centre, and over the heads of the front riders. T'was a gravel road (no black top in those times) and full of potholes. The gig being sprung, lurched, bucked, and bounced, and if ever there was a reason to get seasick on dry land this surely was it. The neighbour, scared witless, clutched, grabbed and tried to keep his hat on all at the one time. "Jesus Mary and Joseph, stop, stop, let me off, we'll all be kilt", he pleaded. Another crack of the whip as we reached the bottom was the answer. Urged on to greater effort the cob broke into a gallop. We were heading towards the local village not a mile away. Rounding a bend leading into the village we were confronted with a T-junction not a hundred yards away. A few locals had gathered on the patch of grass at the junction and they must have thought they were witnessing a Roman chariot race, with passengers! Wisely they scattered. Like a modern day joy rider Father left the breaking till the last moment, then, hauling back on the reins the cob slid to a halt, executed a tight turn, and was off back in the direction we had come from. Everyone, had a different slant on what they had seen, and it kept them in conversation for the rest of the summer. Some said it was a genuine run-a-way, and t'was lucky no one got kilt. Others thought the passenger up front was a corpse, no one living could look that white, while some said t'was the Divil himself that held the reins!

On the homeward journey the cob settled into a good fast clip that any owner could be proud of and the neighbour's nerves had settled enough to take notice of it. There was one other facet to the episode that added a flavour to the evening. The cob coming off a lush pasture had a bellyful of green grass in him, and he farted practically the whole way there and back leaving well scattered globs of loose green horseshit all along the gravel road. The smell lingered in the evening air long after the dust had settled.

Arriving back in the farmyard the cob was unhitched and the original animal put back between the shafts. "All that cob needs is plenty of work," was the terse comment and there was no reply. A proud stubborn man, the neighbour was between a rock and a hard place. Several locals had witnessed the village scene and he knew the stories that would float. He wasn't going to have it said by all and sundry that he couldn't handle a lively animal. Like a man who spends most of his life driving a sedate 1.5 litre saloon and then decides to buy a hotted up 2 litre + job he'd have to become acquainted to a faster life style!

We all at some time or other meet our Waterloo and Father's came in the shape of a bay mare called Hilda. She was a tall rangy animal over sixteen hands, and she glided over the ground like a will-o-the wisp her hooves barely tipping the surface. Nothing in the locality could outpace her either on highway or hunting field. It was love at first sight. This one was not for sale, not at any price. But Hilda had one fatal flaw,—she was a jibber. It didn't matter at what stage of the journey, coming, going, or half way either way, if Hilda decided to stop that was that. No amount of coaxing or urging would shift her. A crack of the whip, a belt of the yard brush, gentle cooing and whistling, no dice. Just toss her head and kick was her answer to all kinds of persuasion. Another tactic of hers was to go into reverse and keep reversing until she backed into something. That didn't do anything for the appearance or shape of the gig that she was yoked to and it was dangerous, for once or twice she backed into a ditch. All hands on board had to bail out in hurried fashion. Eventually, he had a special long shafted buggy made for her, the shafts being sixteen feet long. She could kick away to her hearts content, but the buggy bottom remained intact.

On one occasion, Father decided to take Mother and

youngest offspring, aged about five, to see her relatives and stay overnight. The distance was 'round twenty miles and as Mother hadn't seen her relations for quite some time she was looking forward to meeting up again and made preparations for the weekend. They were as nothing compared to the preparations made to try and ensure a safe and sure take off! All gates to the road wide open for swift exit. Hilda harnessed and lunged in a field to warm her up. The long shafted buggy moved manually to the field into which Mother climbed aboard and waited, with a considerable amount of anxiety. There was no way she was going to let her youngest in with her until 'move off' looked reasonably safe. That manoeuvre had yet to be worked out. When hook up time arrived it went without a hitch, and Hilda started off in her long loping stride, (she never walked). To load Junior the plan was simple. Father started circling Hilda in ever decreasing circles, my sister and I with a firm grip on brother's arms and ankles awaited the precise moment. There was nothing precise about the delivery, he was flung into the back of the buggy with a lot of effort on our part and a great deal of luck They set off and Hilda never broke stride, up hill and down dale till they arrived at their destination in a record breaking time of one hour and twenty five minutes. They returned safe and well next day without a hitch, and thereafter the neighbours chided Father that it was the feminine influence that caused Hilda's good behaviour. Maybe there was something in it for my Mother was a gentle woman, but only Hilda knew the real reason, and she never told anyone! Eventually she was sold to a lady for hunting; the money was small. Hilda was I suppose his greatest disappointment in horse circles, but he did have one or two other notable successes. He bred and broke a winner of the Scottish Grand National, and had a mare that bred four fillies who each in their turn won the same race in four consecutive years. As far as I know that record still stands.

He went to the Happy Hunting Land in the mid 50's and a large cross section of the racing and hunting fraternity among many others turned out for his funeral. As the grave was filled in people stood around in groups swapping yarns and anecdotes, reliving memories. A near neighbour listening in summed it all up with a simple comment, —"Sure he had horse blood in his veins!"

Chapter 6
The Dismal Fifties

The 1950's were a stagnant decade in rural Ireland. Only towards the end of it did agriculture get a bit of a move on, but as it was still a major player in the Irish economy you could say that the whole country was in neutral.

With the war over, across the water and all Europe was going hell for leather in a recovery boom. Houses and factories were going up apace, highways were being built, gas mains and all services laid. New regiments were formed shouldering shovels not rifles, Wimpy's foot solders, MacAlpine's fusiliers. A plentiful supply of manpower and food were needed and as cattle and people were still our greatest exports Ireland was able to fill some of that need.

Here in Ireland we were not too upset by the stagnation; we were too busy slapping ourselves on the back. "Weren't we the great little nation entirely, keeping out of trouble for nigh on five year with a ready market for all our cattle, sons, and daughters, and if a-self, Molly, Johnny, Mary and Joe had to go work for the auld inemny didn't she pay well, and didn't she owe it to us anyroads, and sure the few pounds sent home didn't go astray." As for progress in farming, "Didn't me father set a good headline, an' if I follow in his footsteps sure I couldn't go far astray." Looking over the ditch at the fella next door makin' a fist of it wasn't a bad headline either. It could be called 'Thirty's Thinking' and that's about where we were in the early '50's. Yes, tractors did appear on the horizon in greater numbers, but a lot of them were hitched to horse drawn implements. You could buy a new one for around £500, but if you wanted to equip it fully with its own implements, plough, cultivator, seeder etc, you were getting in deep financially speaking. £500 was a lot of dough in those days and if you could scrape up that amount sure didn't you have a few implements already that it could pull. A three part horse harrow, horse carts with the shafts taken off and a short pole fitted for a drawbar made a trailer. It was the same with hay mowers and binders. It was a start; with a bit of luck and a good year one could trade up. Slowly but surely horse ploughs and the like were consigned to headlands and haggards, there to rust away amidst nettles and briers. Few thought that one day those discarded pieces of equipment would double their value as antiques! It was a case of 'good riddance'.

But all was not doom and gloom. Information for the betterment of farming and farmers started to trickle through from various sources. The formation of the NFA, now IFA, Macra, the arrival of livestock marts pushing the old fairs into the background till they eventually faded away, the Farmers Journal (Fearlessly on the Farmers side). All these played their part in the pooling and sharing of ideas. The major source of information and advice in those early days were the County Committees of Agriculture, later known as ACOT and now-a-days Teagas. Their field officers could be seen roaming the fields auger in one hand and soil sample cartons in the other taking soil samples to be sent away to Johnstown Castle to be tested for N.P. & K (nitrogen, potash, and phosphate). When the results from these samples were applied, you could say that grass and cereal crops literally lepped out of the ground.

These same men held seminars and lectures in parochial halls and hotel function rooms all over the country, showing slides and giving talks on all aspects of farming. Out went the dual - purpose cow, in came the high producing milker (Friesian). The scrub bull went over the hill, not entirely, but stockowners were advised and admonished to upgrade their bulls and rams, various sheep breeders associations also played their part. Cereal growers were fed the results of field trials on various cereal and root crops tested on the Department of Agriculture farms. Farm walks were also encouraged on the said farms. Agriculture was awakening, no longer was the attitude, "T'was good enough for me father, t'will be good enough for me" acceptable. Banks, those wonderful institutions who pass out umbrellas when the sun is shining sat up and took notice; careful loans were arranged! The ACC (Agriculture Credit Corporation) was spawned and hung out its "Open for Business" sign. This caused the other entrenched institutions to huff and puff and lower your loan a percentage point when negotiating with them.

Two of the major motivators of the time were the Land Reclamation and Lime Spreading schemes plus grant and subsidy. A subsidy tacked onto any scheme makes a farmer sit up and pay attention. It's looked on as a sort of luck penny and a luck penny sweetens any deal. Irish men, who were in the heavy equipment business in England packed their bags, put their machines on the boat and got stuck in over here in double quick time. Bulldozers, which started life building aerodromes in England were soon to be seen knocking out double ditches and big hawthorn hedges in Ireland. Draglines, (Hi-Mac's and Back-Actors) flung mud and rushes out of drains, that hadn't been cleared since the day of dot. Land that was once waterlogged and considered only fit for grazing was soon producing crops of wheat. I should add that not all operators came from England, some of them started from scratch here.

It was a money making scheme for all, for it was hardly under way when farmers realised that not only could they get their land cleared and drained, but they could make a few pounds out of it as well. It worked something like this. After application was made the first man on the scene was the man from the Department. He surveyed the land, wrote down figures in his book, went back to the office and having decided the project was viable gave the go ahead on a piece of paper setting out what was to be done and the amount of grant the Department was prepared to put towards it. The grants were generous. Smart operators soon realised that they could do the job for the grant, and at no cost to the farmer. Wonderful, but ugly competition reared its head and a cost cutting exercise came into effect. Everyone had climbed on the bandwagon and everyone wanted to stay on board. It was money for auld rope. Project officers were almost run over by drainage operators seeking the names of those who had an application in, and then a mad dash to the farmyard to tell the farmer that they could not only do the job for the grant, but at something less. Manys the bewildered farmer found himself doing a deal for a job not yet cleared by the Dept, but the thoughts of a few pounds left over for himself soon settled his nerves. Maybe the grants were overgenerous, but the end result was spectacular. Production almost doubled.

Then came a year that caused a temporary 'hick up' to all this activity. "One more sow, one more cow, one more acre under the plough" was the slogan at the time and the sitting Minister of Agriculture decided to do something about the acre bit. He figured that the boar and bull would attend to the other two! With great fanfare and vote catching ability, he announced that for every barrel of wheat produced that year (1954) the farmer would receive £4 per barrel for it. It was an unheard of price; the ploughs were out immediately and the green fields of Ireland blackened with turned over sods. Con-acre (rented land) made £20 an up per acre, land that hadn't been ploughed since famine times was turned over.

It was one of those years that could best be described as a 'droppin' year', no shortage of rain, and the crops grew lush and tall. Come harvest time Mother Nature took a hand and we had one of the wettest harvests on record. Some fields were never harvested, and sacks of wheat could be seen all over the country lying rotting where they were dropped off the combine, green sprouting wheat showing through the fibre's of the sack. Wild duck and geese flying south couldn't believe their luck; grain and water, their staples, were in abundance for most of Ireland was a slob land. Some fields showed a unique quality for retaining water; small lakes and ponds remained up to damn near Christmas. I don't know what the cost was to the Exchequer or the miller, but paying £4 for a barrel of wheat with 25% to 30% water in it couldn't have been cheap, and it certainly tightened manys a farmer's purse strings. Some swore they'd "let it out to grass and go back to the bullock", if it rained a-self, he, the bullock, had the privilege of standing under the hedge!

But one bad year doesn't put a halt to a farmers gallop and the main job progressed. When the clearing and draining were completed the crème-de-la-crème was applied. Lime, tons of it, for a lot of Irish soil was sadly lacking that essential ingredient to make crops flourish. Billowing clouds of lime dust drifted across the countryside as two ton spreaders moved up and down fields distributing their loads. Tractors with front-loaders waited on the headlands to re-fill them and housewives rushed to their clotheslines to retrieve the washing! If you were unlucky enough to get behind a lime truck on a crooked narrow road your windscreen took on an opaque hue, the car, regardless of its original colour turned a greyish white.

Not all progress took place on the arable lowlands where trucks, tractors, and spreaders could manoeuvre with relative ease. The men with mountain farms were quick to catch on, for they too could see that a patch of ground no matter how small was better growing grass than bracken or gorse, but there was a snag, accessibility. Some of these 'hard to get at areas' were reached with the small 5cwt mounted fertiliser spinners mounted on the back of small tractors. But what about the areas that were unreachable? Well to my knowledge, there were two fellows who didn't give it a second thought. Tho' living thirty miles apart and not known to one another they had two things in common, grit and determination. Both owned small mountain farms. The fact that the two pieces of ground (they could hardly be described as fields) could best be described as standing on their ends, did not deter these two gladiators.

The first patch of ground needed ploughing, so it was attacked with a two-sod plough attached to the rear of a TVO Ferguson. To get to the summit was a hazardous journey. Conventional steering was almost non-existent for the front wheels had minor contact with the ground and had to be assisted with the aid of the independent brakes on each rear wheel. Arriving at the summit ploughing was one way only,—downhill. The steepness of the hill sometimes caused the rear sod to fly up in the air like a whiplash instead of settling down snugly beside its partner the front sod. When it came to cultivating a pin harrow was rigged up behind a grubber to cut down on travel time, thus creating the first one pass system of sorts that is so in vogue on tillage farms today.

The next hurdle was to move thirty tons of limestone from farmyard to summit. It travelled sack full by sack full, half of the journey on the back of the tractor, the other half on the back of the gladiator, to be dumped on the ground in small heaps then scattered 'round be shovel', not mechanical!

The second piece of ground was similar, tho' not needing ploughing and maybe a shade smaller. Twenty six tons of lime was involved and the same problem faced the second gladiator, transportation from site to summit. Maybe he had a bad back, but if so, he certainly had strong arms and shoulders, for he elected to move it by bucket. Slowly but surely, bucket full by bucket full; he moved the pile two buckets at a time spreading each one by hand when he got there. He lived to the ripe old age of ninety six. The neighbours said he died of hardship, but if he did a-self, he sure gave hardship a run for its money!

And so the Dismal 50's dragged to a close. Agriculture was awake but barely out of bed. Since those times it has moved in leaps and bounds to become one of the most efficient industries in the country in terms of output per man unit. With agriculture, radio, and computer technology growing apace, will we soon be looking at the 'nine to five farmer'? Yes, just as soon as we can get a 'nine to five cow'!

Chapter 7
EEC

A new dawn for agriculture arose when eventually Ireland signed up for EEC membership in 1973. Agriculture advisors swarmed over the countryside urging farmers to produce, produce, produce, and telling us how to do it with new and better methods. Seminars and lectures were held in hotel conference rooms, pub lounges, and the various County Committee of Agriculture offices. The meetings were packed; learning was at a premium. In fairness to the Department of Agriculture and their Advisors, they had been around for a decade or more but their knowledge got scant attention. "Dem advisor lads, they'd break ya", was the consensus of earlier times, now, the possibility of earning real money was the driving force that filled the meeting halls.

Farmers weren't the only ones to be affected by this itch. Bank managers awaited eagerly in their plush offices for that 'hoped for' appointment. Protocol deterred them from actually standing in the doorway to smilingly greet you, but the charm was turned on when arriving in the 'inner sanctum'. Land was the new investment. Just to be sure, to be sure, banks hired their own agriculture advisors! There was another breed not affected by protocol who jumped on the bandwagon. Up laneways and down boreens the 'hail fellow well met' agriculture salesman greeted one and all. Back in the Thirties and Forties little enough trading was done in agricultural machinery. A new plough, harrow, or seed drill, could be purchased from any good hardware shop, which also handled all other farm necessities. Tractor sales and their ancillary equipment in the Forties Fifties and Sixties were usually handled by an existing car dealership garage. But in the Seventies and on into the Eighties the specialisation age was upon us, and so it is to this very day. Agricultural tractors and agricultural machinery come to us now from all over Europe and specialised dealerships have been set up to service them.

Bumbling bureaucracy took a hand when we first entered the EEC For once it was to the farmers advantage. We were supposed to enter in an orderly fashion; prices for agriculture products were to rise by 8% per year for ten years or visa versa I've forgotten which. That way we would build gradually up to European prices, but the guys doing the sums at 'head office' got it wrong. Apparently their calculations showed an adequate supply of foodstuffs. The reality was a scarcity. The inevitable happened, the law of supply and demand took over, prices almost doubled overnight. Cattle prices especially. In the wink of an eye a beast worth fifty pounds rose to the dizzy height of one hundred pounds. Bonanza time had arrived. The sting in the tail came when one went to restock; a lot of the gain went into the replacement animal. But not to worry, inflation was rampant, money was useless. To have stock on the land gaining value while they grazed was smart investment. Another good buy was land. In the mid Fifties land value was about £33 per acre (e40.90), by the early Seventies it had passed the £1000 mark (e1269.74). When small pockets of land between two farms came up for sale it was a battle royal between the two neighbours each determined to add it to their existing holding.

Through the Seventies and on into the Eighties nobody paid much heed to the stockpile of perishable farm produce that continued to grow and grow, eventually becoming beef and butter mountains, milk and wine lakes. The quick fix answer was to build more cold stores. A new service industry had sprung up! They were hardly completed when food was at the door waiting to get in. Efforts were made to sell it on, but frozen food two years old is not very attractive. Floor prices were offered from Russia and some North African countries for beef and butter well past their sell by date, but still the rush to fill the cold stores continued. A game of musical chairs or pass the parcel between cold stores started up in their efforts to find space. Frozen meat from a midlands store would head to a store in the south returning with a load of frozen butter from the southern store, which had to be moved to make room for the load of meat! The more adventurous loads moved between countries. A trucker having unloaded at a cold store in Paris say, could get orders from his boss to reload there, and bring a load to a store somewhere in England. It was all grist to the mill and everyone was making money!

Part of the problem was caused by Ministers for Agriculture of the EU member states coming home from meetings in Brussels with continued good news for their farmers. Another penny or two on milk, a pound or so per ton on grain or sugar beet drove farmers to greater efforts. Food stocks piled up! In the beef sector alone, intervention prices, originally designed to put a floor price under beef, became the best price. Naturally, meat factories took advantage of this situation, killing everything that was offered and shoving it into cold storage. Scant attention was paid to grading, quality control, or more important marketing. The cold store was the only market and the money was government backed. Some factories did make the effort to get onto supermarket shelves with considerable success.

The law of supply and demand kick started us on our entry into the EU, now it would work against us. With mountains and lakes of food piled up all over Europe there was an adequate sufficiency for all, and nobody wanted the surplus except at give away prices. With the dogs in the street having a bark about it, the bureaucrats at 'head office' awoke, took a big yawn, and decided that something would have to be done. But what? No matter what decision was to be taken it was going to be painful for farmers. Slash prices was the only and obvious one. With one stroke of a pen farmer's dreams of eternal wealth came to an abrupt halt. The clarion call to 'intensify' that had carried them onwards for neigh on twenty years suddenly became a dirty word. A replacement one was sought and found,-- 'extensify'. It's an ironic fact, but the new philosophy in agriculture seems to be taking us back to the Hungry Thirties. In those days land was valued by the number of acres it took to carry a cow or bullock. Two acres to a cow was considered good land, five, poor land. At the height of intensification land was expected to carry 18/20 cwt per acre, (two ten cwt bullocks). With extensification now in vogue we are creeping back to the two acres per cow! Another similarity appearing is the inability of average sized farms to sustain a liveable income for the farmer and his family. Back in those poor times men on small acres had to work outside their holding to make ends meet. Today the farmer's wife is quite likely to be a working mother, (schoolteacher, physiotherapist, nurse) and the man himself is working extra hours with Farm Relief, or doing a bit of outside contracting. There is a difference in that nowadays farmers are collecting grants and subsidies on animals and acres, which were not available in the Thirties. These monies can amount to over 50% of a farmer's income; not a good system. We have gone full circle and are back to square one!

Chapter 8
The Fordson Tractor

My Father was considered to be a progressive farmer, so it seemed natural that one of the first tractors in the area was on our farm, and to be the son of a farmer who had a tractor in those days added a certain status among his school peers. At least that is how it appeared to a ten year old and upwards! To mention casually "one was hurrying home from school to give the tractor man a break from the ploughing" was social climbing of the highest order. There was an element of truth in the proud boast. Yes, I did hurry home when the tractor was working, and after shovelling a slice of bread and glass of milk down my throat was out to the field where it was working, to sit on the wide mudguard riding up and down the field watching the wheels relentless turning, that, and the two grass sods flying from the boards of the plough being turned upside down to lie side by side matching the two sods that had being turned from the previous round. It was a pastime I never tired of, and when the driver, a fellow called Dinny Graham, let me sit on the seat and steer up and down the field my joy knew no bounds. No power steering in those days so help was needed when turning on the headland!

Having almost reached the ripe old age of sixteen I considered myself a capable tractor driver and at about the same time my father traded in the blue tractor for a new yellow one, which soon developed a growl in its rear end. Being still under guarantee Father instructed me to drive it back to the garage from whence it had being purchased. Duthie Large was the garage and was located in the town of Athy about twenty miles south of our place. The journey suited me fine for I still suffered from a ten year olds mentality when it came to showing off my driving prowess, and here was a golden opportunity to show off in front of complete strangers whom I might meet or pass along the way! Barrelling along that straight stretch of road between the Moate of Ardscull and Athy, or put another way 'flat out at ten m p h', I spied a figure approaching, leading a bicycle. As we drew nearer to each other the figure halted, as if taking a rest; to asses the situation might have been nearer the mark, for the figure in question was none other than a Civic Guard as the Gardá were called in those days. Also in those days there was a distinct mark of respect for such people in authority! Previously along the way I had waved cheerily and smiled cheekily at other road users, but this situation called for different tactics. It was a case of 'mind your P's and Q's', which consisted mostly of driving correctly, and be on your own side of the road. The speed limit was not a worry; ten mph could hardly be described as break neck speed or driving in a dangerous manner, not on the open road anyway. The distance between us was down to a hundred yards or so when he moved the bike out onto the middle of the road, then, horror or horrors he stretched high his arm. It could only mean one thing; I was been requested to halt, for there was only the two of us on that long lonely stretch of a mile or more of road. Shutting down the hand throttle and knocking her out of gear I made the perfect three-point landing coming to a halt right beside the guardian of the law. It's a long time ago but the conversation went something as follows. "Well, young fella" was his opening remark I didn't know the meaning of the word obsequious at the time but I know I tried hard to look it. An where would ye be going?" "Athy, Sir", I replied. "Umm, Athy is a big place, any place in particular ye were thinkin' a goin'?" "Duthie Large, Sir, ya see, she's got a growl in her rear end". His glance indicated that I might be trying to be a 'smart ass' but satisfied that I wasn't, he continued with his line of questioning in proper garda mode. "Do ye drive much?" Puffed up with vanity I failed to see where this line of questioning was going. "Yes Sir," I answered boastfully, I do most of the drivin' at home. This was partially true. "Ye'd be needin' a licence with all that drivin'", was his next trusting remark! Too late, I realised where this line of questioning was heading. "Could I be seein' yer license", he asked deadpan. "I don't have one", I blurted out. He undid the button on the top pocked of his tunic and pulled out a notebook and stub of pencil. "What did ye say yer name was". He hadn't asked originally, but I suppose it was a polite way of speaking to the condemned. By now I was in a blue funk and my imagination in overdrive. What was the penalty for no driving licence? Six weeks, six months, or six years? Slowly he copied down all particulars, then satisfied that I had told the truth the whole truth and nothing but the truth he let me continue my journey. Father was sometime later summoned to the District Court in Naas and fined ten shillings for allowing a juvenile drive a vehicle on a public road without a driving license. We lived in simple times!

When today's farmer goes to buy a tractor he has a wide choice, not only of make, but also of model, and even each model has its choice and range of services to offer. Tailored made to suit your own special requirements. Fifty odd years ago, your choice was mainly limited to colour, blue or yellow, for the make and model was pretty standard, and if the dealer sent word that the tractor you'd ordered six months ago was ready for delivery you didn't enquire what colour it was. There were other makes, David Brown and Marshall come to mind, but the Fordson was the popular choice when you had no choice. It was a blue Fordson. The model is now a collector's item so it deserves a special mention.

She weighed in at 3000 lbws (minus driver), was 24 horsepower (4380cc) and ran on T. V. O. (paraffin oil). No comfort cab, no power steering, no lights, no self starter. Ignition was supplied, according to the maker, by a high tension magneto with impulse coupling for easy starting. Those last three words brought manys' a caustic comment from owners and drivers on a frosty morning! I only ever heard the one retort repeated many times over on such mornings, and in my youthful innocence thought that, that was the reason why tractors were always referred to in the feminine gender. It was short and cryptic "Ya bitch." She also came with a very comprehensive instruction book and if you felt so inclined you could take her all to pieces and put her back together again, every step explained in great detail. I don't think many farmers availed of the D I Y offer! You could have carbon removed and valves ground for 30 shillings, decarb only

12/6, and if you buggered up the crankshaft you could have it straightened for only 7/6. A new fan belt fitted and adjusted 3 shillings Need I say more!

Regardless of which gender you care to place the Fordson in, it was a reliable machine, if at times a temperamental one, and most times it's temperament was governed by the treatment meted out to it by over exuberant, but under knowledged plough mechanics. We Irish are a resourceful people and look forward to a challenge. We also have an amazing ability to tinker, (fiddle with), and the less we know about something the more eager we are to tinker.! Last week in charge of 2 horsepower, this week in charge of 24. It was a challenge no self respecting Irishman could refuse and being an adaptable people we dropped the reins and grabbed the steering wheel like a duck to water. From National school (primary) drop- outs to middle aged men who had spent a lifetime walking behind a pair of horses everyone was eager to have a go, given half a chance. It was the beginner who saw the temperamental side of the Fordson. Compared to the diesel engine of today, there were several things to go wrong. A good damp Irish morning caused condensation on plugs, plug leads, and magneto points, three items in the sparks division alone. Carburettor flooding, leading on to plugs sooting / oiling up. The tractor was started on petrol and when warmed up was switched over to T.V O.(tractor vaporising oil) i.e. paraffin. Too quick a change over also caused plugs to soot up. All simple things to the knowledgeable one, and easy to correct, but for the beginner with a desire to tinker it was a mystery trail causing endless time lost and deep frustration. Following a definite line of enquiry was usually more luck than logic Very often when she would eventually cough into life the sweat stained crank swinger (man on starting handle) would be unsure as to what he had done to achieve such a spectacular result. By trial and error you eventually got your degree!

At the other end of the scale, was the Know- All, who liked nothing better than an audience when something went wrong. An opportunity to show off his mechanical know -how. We had such a fellow on our place. He was nicknamed the Badger, which had nothing to do with his mechanical skills, but he was reputed to have kept badgers tied to the end of his bed for badger baiting at the weekends. A cruel sport that was popular in those times. The badger was set upon by fighting dogs, one at a time to see who would come off best in the fight. The badger didn't stand much chance for he would have several opponents, all eager to take their chances. I never did know if the story was true or false but the nickname stuck.

If perchance he was working in a field that was bounded by the public road at one end, he would always stop at the road headland to carry out some minor adjustment in the hope that some passer-by would stop to bid the time of day and enquire as to the trouble. The passer-by in those days could be some fellow droving a few sheep and taking them easy, and a half hour chat would rest the sheep and help pass the time. Or it could be some fellow taking his bike for a walk; on his way home from the local pub- grocery; a shopping bag draped over the handlebars of the bike and a couple a pints inside him, hence the reason for walking and the need for a rest. He'd always wanted to get a close up look at one of them new fangled yokes that was coming into the country and here was one right over the ditch from him. The bike would be laid down on the grass verge and he'd squeeze through the hedge. "Are ya bruk down"? "No, just cleanin' the points". "Aye, I suppose that has to be done to". The only "points" yer man has any knowledge of is the ones inside him, but no matter, he leans over to get a better look. Mister Know- All (Badger) now has a captive audience and goes into great detail explaining how these points open and close creating a spark which runs up the plug leads to the plugs and fires the engine into action. Yer man is spellbound, and gazes intently at those two little points hardly believing what he has heard. Back in the pub that night where he has gone to top up the couple he had during the day, he too holds a captive audience. Like a Yale lecturer he speaks with authority on the merits and marvels of magneto points. "I tell yis no lie, two little bits a yolkes no bigger ner the head of a match". All go home at closing time, or near enough, satisfied with the knowledge that the magneto is the heart of an engine. An so it is!

Badger also had a mean little trick which he played on the unsuspecting whenever he got the chance. Could be one of them damp Irish mornings (raining stair rods) when a spark plug or two would need drying out before the engine would kick into life. To day, drying out plugs would be a simple matter. Borrow the wife's hair dryer and blow the hot air over the plugs and all would be well in jig time, but in those days it took longer. Each plug had to be taken out and dried individually, usually with a pocket handkerchief or maybe a piece torn off the inside lining of a top coat. The piece of rag would then be dampened with a drop of petrol, set fire to, and all the plugs placed on it like four pieces of kindling wood on a fire there to dry properly and warm up. All this took time, and as the rain hadn't yet cleared off the rest of the farm staff would have gathered 'round to offer advice or just plain look on, passing the odd comment on when the weather was likely to clear. A newcomer to the staff or a servant boy would be the target for Badger's trick. "Here, lay your hand to that a minute," he'd say, passing a plug lead to the eager innocent. With all plugs out there'd be no compression and Badger would give a quick crank on the starting handle. As a 100 volts or thereabouts shot through his body the captive would let out a yell, jump off the ground and grab his wrist thinking maybe it was broken. Guffaws of laughter all 'round. Badger with a dead pan look on his face would say "What's da matter, did she give ya a bit 'iv a tickle." ?

With all her contrary ways, the easiest one of all to cure was nearly always the last one to be checked. There was a drain cock on the bottom of the carburettor and if opened and no fuel appeared it was immediately assumed that 1 the float was stuck, or 2 there was dirt somewhere, thus causing a fuel blockage. Having dismantled the carburettor and examined the float and needle minutely and finding nothing amiss, it might then dawn on the tinkerer to unscrew the fuel tank cap and take a peek inside. Empty! The thought process that caused this to happen over and over again has always eluded me.

A neighbour once purchased a second hand Fordson and three men were dispatched to load it onto a truck to bring it home. A suitable bank was found to more or less equal the height of the truck body. No low loaders with loading ramps in those days Planks were laid from bank to body. I should perhaps explain why all this was taking place. The tractor was owned by a fellow called the Plumber, who was anxious to see the back of her because some of her temperamental. ways had become a bit chronic. A deal had been struck previously, £200 pounds asked, a £150 bid, final price £170, nothing more to be done but load up. The truck driver, the only one of the gang who knew what he was about, elected to drive her on. The Plumber whispered to him anxiously not to let her stall or stop till she was safe aboard. The critical moment was when the weight of the tractor transferred from plank to truck. The driver, been a careful sort of fellow, eased off the throttle a mite. She coughed, spluttered, and the engine died. A "puttuff" from the exhaust seemed to say she had given up the ghost and had no plans to go further. The Plumber took command with alacrity, "We'll push her the rest-a the way Lads, no trouble at-all". Horsepower converted into manpower and with much heaving, pushing, and grunting she was nudged aboard. On arriving at home base another suitable bank was found for the unloading. A gallery had gathered, for all wanted a gawk at this mechanical wonder. There was to be no lowering of standards, no pushing and heaving in front of the home team. What was the use of having 24 horsepower sitting there looking at you, let her drive off under her own steam. There was plenty of young muscle standing around eager to have a go at the starting handle. She took 'em all on, but refused to start. Coats off, chests heaving, sweat stained faces, they stood around in a huddle wondering what the next move might be. Naturally, there was no shortage of suggestions. One fellow allowed that she might be low in water. The truck driver, in a patient manner informed him that a water shortage in the radiator had no bearing on getting her started, but the remark did have further consequences. Knowing there was nothing for it only take out the spark plugs and dry them, the driver proceeded to do so. When he had them all out he cranked over the engine a few times. This was done to clear any excess fuel out of the cylinders to prevent the plugs from oiling up again, but only he knew the object of the exercise. Quickly noting, that the engine was easily cranked when the plugs were out, someone in the gallery suggested that it might be a bright idea to crank her first and put the plugs in after. A withering look of derision from the driver stopped any more advice from that quarter

With plugs clean and dry and timing checked she started on the first pull and ran sweetly. The driver decided wisely to leave her run awhile and warm up proper so all retired to the house for a cup a tay! On returning to the scene to prepare for drive off the tractor was still running merrily, but had bursts of steam forcing its way out from around the radiator filler cap and puffs coming from the overflow pipe. The fellow with the water suggestion earlier on was delighted with himself, at least he was half right. Feeling vindicated, he proceeded to unscrew the cap shouting for someone to "get a bucket a water". On the last tread the cap blew, not only out of his hand but thirty feet up in the air and came down in a large apple tree covered in ivy never to be seen again. She was driven off the truck in style and thereafter spent many useful hours driving a thrashing mill at harvest time and a grain crusher and turnip pulper in winter. Someone passed the remark at the time, "she was a good buy."

The Fordson era came to a close 'round the end of the 40's early 50's and are now collectors items. It was replaced by the Fordson Major (I think) the first of the "tall" tractors and then the Ford Major and so on to today's models, the only retaining resemblance being the colour, blue. As I said at the beginning today's farmer has a wide option on what make or model he wants, but lets not forget the old "squat" Fordson and other makes, which were the first to get us out of the horse age and into the age of mechanisation.

Chapter 9
The Ferguson TE 20

Another piece of machinery that helped revolutionized farming was the TE 20 Ferguson tractor, for it introduced hydraulics into the farm tractor. In farming parlance, the threepoint linkage, there by improving traction, accessibility, manoeuvrability and giving us those two great inventions,—the front end loader and pick-up hitch. Previous tractors were nothing more than mechanical draught horses, very often in greasy conditions concentrating all their horsepower on digging two large holes in the ground with their rear wheels while the implement they were meant to be pulling sat there mutely looking on. A quick up and down flick of the lift lever on the TE 20 usually got you out of such situations.

Mind you, there was no immediate rush to flood Irish farms with them. We Irish farmers are a cautious lot, and it took a lot of looking over the ditch before decisions were taken. “How’s she goin’?” “Begor, she’s a great little yoke altogether.” This sort of publicity given free gratis was the sort of advertisement that any salesman could only dream about. The rush was on. Machinery dealers, some who hardly knew the front from the back of a tractor, couldn’t get them out fast enough. They suited the small to medium sized farm down to a tee. There was of course the odd hitch as is normal for any item so revolutionary. The following tale, which involved me personally, relates one such temporary hick-up.

Harry Ferguson was not only practical he was also clever. He wanted his tractors to be self-sufficient, and manufactured an implement for every occasion and job. In other words, once the tractor was purchased it was the start to the purchase of a range of implements, all suited to his tractor. Mind you, he wasn’t up to the ingenuity of some farmers who cobbled up various arrangements to save their pockets! One of these implements was the 3 row ridger. Designed to put up drills for root crops, with a little care and a great deal of practice it worked well. But when it came to splitting the drills for covering spuds, that’s when the ridger produced a mind of its own. Your lovely straight drills became a series of S bends, and the spuds you were meant to cover sat up and looked at you, naked to the elements. You cursed and swore and in a fit of rage demanded from your dealer to send out that ‘Demonstration Fella’. At this stage I might add, that every implement came with a detailed instruction book. It was consigned to the top of the kitchen dresser on the day of arrival, there to remain for all time

The demonstration I write about took place in a poorly ploughed field with a vigorous line of scutch grass growing along each furrow. The plot for the spuds was no more than an acre of ground, and an attempt at drilling was visible! The Fergie sat on the headland with ridger attached. About twelve neighbours stood around, maybe four interested, the rest gawkers,—the hurlers on the ditch! The Demonstration Fella arrived, and apart from a friendly "Hello" to all, didn't waste time. He unhooked from the ridger climbed aboard the Fergie and hit the starter, then reversed up to a nine-tined cultivator, sometimes called a stiff legged grubber. Then horror of horrors he proceeded to cultivate across the furrows of the ploughed land. A cry went up from the onlookers, "Jasus, what's he at?" "He's in right trouble now". It was at the time considered sacrilege to do such an act. It was standard practice to first work along the furrow and when nicely worked down to a fine tilt, then, and then only, work across. "This fella must be from the city," was the opinion of all. "Cripes, he's making a right mess", was another comment, as they watched the grubber tear up sods of clay. The Demonstration Fella blithely carried on crossing and criss-crossing until the lumps and sods broke down into a workable seedbed. He put in a good hour working a small area, which didn't say much for the original ploughman! Finally satisfied with the conditions he unhooked from the grubber, hitched up to the ridger, made a couple of minor adjustments then set off to raise the first drills. The crowd on the headland bunched up watching in anticipation. He reached the far headland, turned, and came back. The drills were as straight as a die. "Be Cripes, that bates all," an onlooker commented. "Hould yer horses," came a retort from another, "just wait till he splits dem." This he proceeded to do to the amazement of all.

He made and split about ten drills, all perfect, then stopped. "Who wants to have a go", he called out cheerily. Some of the crowd took an immediate interest in sheep grazing in the next field others gazed at the ground. There were no takers. They'd come to see that Demonstration Fella make a bollocks of it, and he had confounded the critics. The "It couldn't be done brigade" were in retreat so they looked around for another Fall Guy. Their gaze fell on me! I, the youngest of the crowd having recently returned from foreign fields with boastful tales of deeds accomplished was the obvious choice. "Go on, giv'er a go yerself," words of encouragement came from all directions. With the arrogance of youth on my side I climbed aboard the Fergie. Young and foolish I may have been but I had watched the demonstrator closely, noticing that he had opened the drills shallow, leaving a pathway so to speak on top of each drill. A place to put your wheels when starting to split the drills; more psychological than real, but a help. I was now on the Demonstration Fella's team. "It's no trouble," he said with an assured smile, "Keep her throttled down, and in low gear till you get the feel of it." Throttled down! I nearly stalled on start off. Slowly but surely I moved off. Half way down the field I felt the rear wheels start to slide left. Jabbing hard on the right hand brake pedal I over corrected and she started moving right. A quick jab on the left got me back on course. A quick look 'round and I saw my first S bend. It proved to be the only one, and I started back making better progress, but it's hard to win in front of your own. "Jasus, if he doesn't get a move on it's next years crop we'll be puttin' in."

Nobody else had a go. The day was passing, cows had to be milked other farm chores to be done and the crowd dispersed, but I must have proved some sort of point. I became the local 'Demonstration Fella'!

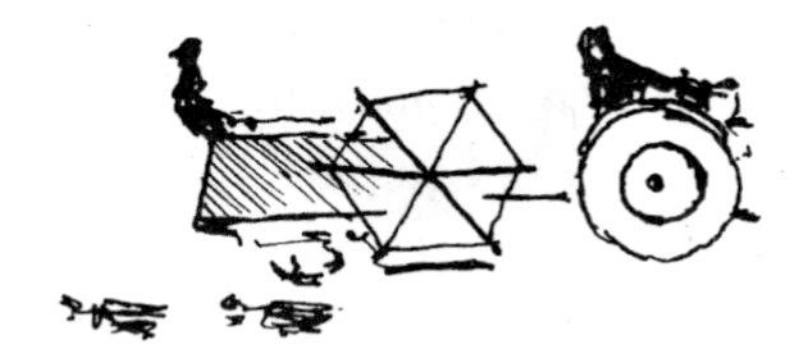

Chapter 10
The Reaper and Binder

Down the ages, farming, like any other industry has benefited from someone's inventiveness, and the arrival of the reaper and binder was just such an example. It bridged the gap between scythe and today's combine harvester, tho' before the arrival of the binder there was a sheaf gathering apparatus attached to the hay mower that produced loose sheaves. However, it was the invention of the sheaf knotter by a man called Cyrus McCormack that swept the binder into prominence.

It was a simple enough machine with all its moving parts driven by a large bull wheel with cleats, tucked underneath the main frame. In simple terms the cut swath landed on a mobile canvas table where it was moved up between two other canvases. They in turn delivered it onto the knotter table there to be snugly tied and then kicked out onto the ground by the kicker forks.

The canvases ran on wooden rollers. The first horse drawn ones had a 5ft cutter bar. With the arrival of the farm tractor the cutter bar length increased up to 10ft, and power drive from the tractor turned the bull wheel into a weight carrier only.

The secret weapon or heart of the machine was of course the knotter. An intricate piece of equipment finely tensioned which when properly adjusted and set up on a test bench worked marvellously, and usually worked well in a good standing crop, but a long tangled crop of barley or oaten straw often tested it. Its biggest test of all was a farmer with a twelve inch screw wrench in his hand, or worse, a hammer and chisel, in his attempt to tighten or slacken the tension on same. It wasn't always the fault of the knotter. During World War 11 or "The Emergency" as it was known here, poor quality twine was often the culprit. Everything would be running smooth, and then suddenly, from the centre of the ball of twine would appear a long line of either very thin or thick twine. No self respecting knotter could handle that sudden change. The obvious thing to do should have been to cut out the offending piece of material, re knot and carry on. But no, immediately the knotter was blamed and heavy handed adjustment took place. If that didn't work, and it usually didn't, the twine tensioner on top of the twine box was adjusted. You now had a three way puzzle. Twine wrong, knotter wrong, tensioner on twine box wrong. The knotter was situated in a fairly confined space and not easily accessible when the only tool you possessed was a twelve inch spanner, hence the necessity to resort to a hammer and chisel. They too had their limitations and it was a hit or miss operation, miss, and a large chunk of skin disappeared off the hand holding the chisel! Blood gushing from the damaged hand attracted every fly in the parish and added to the anguish of the demented mechanic. Eventually, the twine which was the cause of the trouble in the first place, had by now returned to its original size or thickness, and any adjustments made were adjusted back to normal. With the sweating and swearing over, the machine merrily went round and round the crop cutting and kicking our snugly tied sheaves!

When horses were the mode of traction they had to be good. It was hard pulling and very often a fresh pair were introduced after lunch break. Horse flies and all other kinds plagued them, and if you got a stop the flies deserted the high thorn hedges and centred 'round their heads and tails in a black cloud. Stamping, tail switching, heads bobbing up and down, the poor animals were demented and sometimes moved on without instructions from the operator who had to be alive to that possibility, otherwise he was in danger of being run over should he be clearing the blockage at the front of the machine. The arrival of the tractor didn't eliminate the danger of being run over. Sometimes the handbrake was not properly applied!

The operator was kept busy if the crop was uneven or tangled, and a lodged crop was a nightmare. The reel, which guided the crop onto the table, could be lifted up or down forward of back, depending on crop conditions. There was a lever to move the knotter table forward or back, again depending on length of straw, for it was necessary to keep the twine midway on the sheaves. Before start up in the morning knives had to be sharpened, the machine oiled, and the canvases checked for even tension and general wear and tear. Maybe a broken strap or canvas buckle.

Anywhere a gang of men gathered, be it hay or harvest field much good humoured fun was poked at one another. During "The Emergency", already referred to, compulsory tillage was introduced, and old pasture fields were ploughed up that very often were surrounded by big deep ditches, some containing water some dry, but all of them with a dense growth of briers. On the opening round the binder ran close to these ditches and sometimes the odd sheaf would get kicked by the kicker forks straight into them, where it would come to rest on a bed of briers and sink slowly down to the bottom. The tractor driven and operator would take note and smile knowingly at one another, then bide their time. Come tea break the talk would be centred 'round the crop,—was it good, bad, or middlin'. One of the two boyos would pass comment. "Aye, if all the sheaves were got, t'wouln't be a bad crop" Looks all 'round, then the penny would drop. "Anyone check the ditch on the far side?" The slow-witted one or the youngest would be dispatched to check it out, and then get all kinds of encouragement as he struggled to clamber down the steep sides fighting thorny briers all the way down in an effort to retrieve the wayward sheaf.

"Grab a brier, an give yerself a hand"

"Throw her up outa dat".

"What's keepin' ya."

"Get a spade an' we'll bury 'im, he's not cumin up".

The shoe was on the other foot if the crop was tangled and the binder crew were getting lots of stops and hardship. The stookers stood around waiting for sheaves, blowing on their hands and clapping their arms around their bodies as if in arctic conditions.

"Jasus, get a move on, we're persished."

"Are ye waitin' for rain?"

"What d'ya want for Xmas".

It all helped to pass the time I suppose and relieve monotony.

The highlight of the day was when the rabbits started to

bolt. The odd one would leave early, but as the standing crop got smaller and smaller the rest kept moving into the middle of the field. Eventually they had to bolt. Mongrels, half grey hounds, terriers and sheepdogs, men and chaps, all joined in the chase. Rabbits ducked and dived, some running under sheaves thinking they were safe, others trying to make the ditches. Some did others not so lucky. Dogs turned and twisted, men threw sticks and fired forks like spears. If todays animal rights people were present they'd have gone bananas, but a dead rabbit was meat in the pot, and during "The Emergency" would make 1/6 to 2/ shillings each, or 8 to 10 pence in present monies. Humble enough finance but very necessary in those times.

And so the age of the binder has passed, and if you want to see one, your best bet is a farm machinery museum or old photograph. There's still the odd one tucked away on farms here and there, and I know where there's one rusting away in a haggard partially protected by nettles and briers!

Chapter 11
Thrashing

When I achieved the ripe old age of sixteen, Father, on impulse bought a thrashing mill and put me in charge. Not that he said so in so many words, but I think it was his way of recognising youth needing its own independence. On reflection, it was a crafty move on his part. It gave me financial independence, of a sort, and insured that he got his grain thrashed when he wanted it thrashed! The running of a thrashing mill was a two man operation. One to oversee and one to feed the sheaves into the mill, in practice both jobs were interchangeable. The rest of the thrashing crew was the responsibility of the farmer whose grain was being thrashed. The overseer (me) also attended to the financial side of things and plotted the course from farm to farm. This could be a haphazard arrangement. Word of mouth, or in some cases the noise of a thrashing mill in the area would stir a farmer to think about getting his bit done. He would arrive in the haggard during operations, chat to the farmer you were working for, take a walk around and observe how things were going, then make his move.

"She's goin' well," would be a good opening gambit.

"Not bad at all," would be a suitable reply.

"Ye'll be passin' our place when ye're finished here. I've a bit offa days work, I'd say ye'ed knock it out in the day." This put pressure on the overseer, not have him arsing around when and if he set up in this place just down the road! The amount to be thrashed would probably take a day and a half!

"Ye won't be too hard on me," in plain language, this meant how much is this going to cost me. A price would be asked and an offer made. After a bit of haggling a price somewhere in between would be agreed. When the season was over and you made serious efforts to collect monies due quite often more bargaining took place.

If the reaper and binder helped revolutionise the harvesting of grain not only in Ireland but the world over so to did its counterpart, the threshing mill, for in times past they complimented one another. Nowadays they are rolled into one in the form of giant combine harvesters. Fast and efficient with their seventeen foot cutter bars, they move into a field and are finished before they've started it seems. Forty acres cut per day, fifteen / twenty tonnes per hour; unheard of figures in times past. The movement of grain from field to grain store travels in trailers that have increased in size from three tonnes to twenty tonnes. It's all over in a shout, weather permitting of course! Modern technology, in the form of new hybrid grains and improved fertilisers have raised the return per acre; new sprays have reduced diseases and shortened straws, all contributing to the revolution.

Today, if one wanted to see the thrashing behemoths of yesterday one would have to go to a Steam Thrashing Rally. But before the advent of the self propelled combine they were a common sight in Irish haggards in autumn, or rumbling their way from farm to farm, their iron wheels (pneumatics came late) riding in and out of potholes and over stones as big as small potatoes on the gravelled highways of Ireland. The first of them were stationary, driven by stationary steam engines and seen only on large estates or big farms. When the steam engine became mobile, by having a wheel put at each corner with a gearbox added, the two of them cemented a friendship and set off down the byways and lanes of Ireland making themselves available to any farmer who had a bit of grain needing thrashing. It was the first big step towards the modern combine of today. The steam engine was a big cumbersome vehicle soon to be made redundant by the arrival of the farm tractor.

There were many famous makes of thrashing mill; Ransome, Simms, & Jefferies, Marshall, Clayton & Shuttleworth, Garvey, are ones that come to mind. When referring or asking about a mill one always spoke about the size of thrashing drum; thus one spoke about a 4ft Clayton or 4ft Marshall. Manoeuvring these machines along narrow roads and in and out of haggards designed for the horse age took some skill and a great deal of ingenuity. If today you meet a combine on the road there'll be flashing warning lights on it, plus two large wing mirrors keeping the driver aware of what's coming up behind. The old style mirror, was the second part of the crew, sitting on the mudguard of the tractor leaning out at a precarious angle now and again to see it anyone was stuck behind you. If there was, they stayed there, till a crossroads or wide entrance gate gave room for safe passing. The biggest hazard on the road was a steep hill, either up or down. The front part of a mill was mounted on a fore-carriage and the tow bar was connected to same, thus there was no weight on the tractor to aid traction. When tackling a steep hill the helper played a vital part in the event of not reaching the top. To day his title would be 'preventive officer' or some such fancy name. At the bottom, the driver would select a gear he thought suitable for the occasion, then open the throttle wide and charge. With the help of God and a bit of luck you reached the top, black smoke belching from the exhaust, engine pinking, rear wheels half biting half slipping and leaving two very large tracks in the road. The precautionary method used by the helper was a simple one. He ran alongside with a large wooden block in his hands. At the first sign of failure on behalf of the tractor he would throw the block behind one of the mill rear wheels thus preventing a reversal that could have dire results for mill, tractor, and driver. To go down hill was even more hazardous, for when the weight of the mill got pushing on the tractor that jumpy fore carriage was liable to jack knife left or right. Sometimes the centre of the road was not the only way down! The helper not only walked up hills for reasons already mentioned, he also walked down, for someone had to be alive and well when the bottom was reached.

Arriving at the haggard gate was another test of the driver's skill for those gates were very often guarded by two large granite or stone built piers. The gate itself might only be a pole or bed end, but those piers were a formidable challenge. If per chance one of them was damaged the farmer informed you with straight laced face that he had plans to hang gates proper just as soon as he had the money after he'd thrashed, and now he had the added expense of repairing the damaged pier! The intimation was that maybe a few bob would be knocked off the price for thrashing. Added to this nerve wrecking possibility was usually a handful of gawkers; neighbours who has been forewarned of the thrashing and had arrived to give a hand.

If all went according to plan, and on the day, you were full of confidence and felt that God and luck were on your side, you squeezed between those piers and kept going, no stopping till you came up square to the rick or between the ricks that were about to be thrashed. Nods and words of approval all 'round from the men on the fence!

"Some operator."

"One of the best."

"Turn her on a sixpence."

If your luck was out and God had temporarily left your side, and the mill was jammed solid into one of those piers and it looking like the Leaning Tower of Pisa, there were still plenty of words but not of the approving kind.

"Jasus, who let him out?"

"He'd want the next field to turn in."

"Cripes, I wouldn't let him out with a wheelbarrow."

In such a situation it took a lot of jacking, pushing, poling, cursing and swearing, and you might have her free in an hour. There was always lots of free advice; "Whoa," "Go on" "Hold it" "Go up" "Go back," one order countering the other. It called for a cool head! To be fair, a lot of farmers saw the problems and by next season had the gateways widened and some hard core laid down.

The operator and helper were the first to arrive in the mornings for the mill had to be oiled, belts checked, and grain riddles cleaned. With the belt on and mill humming, the help, some of it free and some paid, set to with a will. Casual labour, men without permanent jobs very often followed an outfit from farm to farm hoping for a days pay. A good man was never turned away and would work in a key spot such as pitching the sheaves to the sheaf cutter (often a woman) who in turn passed them to the feeder. A thrashing gang ran from a minimum of eleven to fifteen or maybe eighteen. Too many were as bad as too little for they got in one another's way. A good rick builder was another key man, and as the sheaf rick got smaller and the straw one got bigger help was moved from one to the other. The arrival of the straw elevator was a huge improvement in the handling of straw. Two men were required to handle the sacks, who preferable wore size five hats and thirty six size collars, for a twenty stone (127kg) sack of wheat took some handling if it had to be pushed on a sack truck any distance in soft underground conditions. Sometimes oats for keeping was spread out on a loft, and half sacks were carried on the shoulder up wooden steps. No mean feat. The worst job of all, and for some extraordinary reason, always, it seemed, went to an old man or chap, was keeping the chaff away from under the mill. At the start it was easy enough, for chaff is light, but is practically uncontrollable. Given an unfavourable wind, it was similar to pushing an incoming tide out. Fork, rake, shovel or brush; the instrument to keep chaff away hasn't yet been designed! Along with the chaff was the dust. It hung in the air and got heavier as the day wore on, getting up your nose into your eyes, and into the radiator of the tractor causing it to boil and overheat. A bucket of water fired through the radiator was a quick remedy and a bad one, for the fan behind the radiator turned the water into a fine spray, which was deposited evenly onto the plug leads causing a quick halt to the work. No one minded except the operator, for it was a chance to take your ease and have a smoke while he frantically started drying out the damp leads.

On a good day a hundred and twenty or thirty barrels of wheat or two hundred of barley would be thrashed. Small output by today's standards, but the straw was longer and bulkier and grain yields were less per acre, so I guess that's some of the answer.

The big excitement of the day was when the rick got down to the last few rows of sheaves, and the rats and mice started bolting. Every farm has a dog or dogs and more came with the neighbours. They spent the day growling and snarling at one another and cocking their legs on sacks, wheels, and on your own leg it you didn't watch out, but when the rats started to bolt they closed ranks and went on the attack. Sheep dogs, terriers, mongrels, regardless of breed or size set to with a vengeance. Men with forks, young lads with sticks, some on their way home from school joined in the fray, no quarter given and no prisoners taken. Simple, if somewhat gruesome entertainment. For a brief period the mill ran idle till the battle was over.

Thrashing started round mid September and ran on up to Xmas. There was a bit of Spring work, mostly on the larger farms, but the bulk of it was done in the Fall. The sweet sound of a good running mill, rising and falling as the sheaves were fed into it is a long gone sound from today's autumn/winter air.

I like to go to the odd Steam Thrashing Rally if it's only to stand and listen.

Chapter 12
The Agriculture Contractor

Modern farming has made a niche market for the agriculture contractor. The reasons are simple enough. Scarcity of labour is one reason, every mother with any ambition at all for her son, wants him to go on to third level education and once there he is lost to farm work. But the main reason is economics; in order to stay in business today's farmer has two options, enlarge his holding, not always feasible, or contract out the main farming activities; grain harvesting silage cutting, spraying, fertiliser and slurry spreading etc. Another answer to the problem is to go cooperative with near neighbours. Again this is not always feasible for to be successful the respective holdings have to be of equal size or thereabouts. To sum up, a farm has to be a thousand acres or more to justify investing in machinery that covers all the above mentioned activities, hence the need for the agriculture contractor.

But the agriculture contractor is not an entirely new phenomena; he was always there but could better be described as a part time contractor. In other words, when all the work was tidied up on the home place, the farmer, or more likely his son, would take on off-farm work. A good example would be a son with a mechanical bent. Fresh out of school and anxious to modernise, all he had to do was persuade father to invest in the latest piece of equipment and a bit of 'outside work' would have it paid for in no time! It was also a useful way of earning a few bob for himself.

Fifty years ago the very latest in modern equipment was the combine harvester and the baler. They didn't have an easy passage into Irish agriculture. "They won't work in this country" was the perceived wisdom of the time. "The bales would hate(heat). "Sure they'd go afire in the shed". "Where would ya get the weather in this country to have the hay dry enough for to bale, an if ya did aself sure t'would be all dried up an nothin would ate it." If baled hay had any use at it well sure it might do a few auld stripper cows iv a hard winter, and it was certainly easy to transport around the farm or to other farms. Much agonising took place in pub or at mart, or gawking over hedges to see how the other fella was getting on, as to the pros and cons of baling hay. Slowly but surely the hay baler came to be accepted, if somewhat grudgingly. It was the way to go! The same could be said of the combine harvester, but its advantages could be more readily seen. A huge amount of 'bull work' was eliminated. Stooking, stacking, ricking, the pitching and dragging of sheaves handled at least four times before eventually ending up in a sack was mightily attractive. Nevertheless it did have its complement of begrudgers. Again the weather was a big factor. With the reaper and binder grain could be cut on the rare side; it would ripen and harden in the stook or stack. With the combine it was left to ripen fully on the shank and that's, where lay the problem. "Jasus sure it'll all shed afore ya get to cut it" "What if a windy night comes along, there'll be notin left but the straw". Weeds and a good grassy butt were two factors in the crop that added weight to the arguments of the naysayers. Nowadays modern sprays and earlier ripening grains have eliminated those problems, but they were very big ones when the combine made its first appearance. The operator got over the problem by cutting high and that only gave more food for argument. "Cripes, ye've left half da straw in da field." But in spite of the begrudgers these two machines became accepted into the farming scene. The elimination of hard labour and the speeding up of saving the crop were two very attractive features that eventually won the day.

The operator of either of these two machines faced into minor and major irritations when entering the 'for hire' market, that usually had nothing to do with the saving or harvesting of the crop. Wending his way up narrow boreens with a large machine that were originally designed for an ass and cart, he became part logger part hedge layer. The overhang of alder, ash sucker, and white thorn had to be slashed and cut before arriving at the scene of operations, there to be faced with a field not much more than a few acres. The getting there took up as much time as the actual harvesting and he earned no money for hedge laying! Some of the crop lodged (laying flat on the ground usually due to bad weather or disease in the crop) was another source of haggle between crop owner and operator. When originally approached about doing the job a standard question asked was,—"Is it standing, or lodged"? The answer could be quite evasive. "There might be a bit iv a lodge in the top corner where the wind got at it". The 'top corner' could be near half the field. A lodged crop cut down speed of operation by more than half so a different price had to be negotiated. This often created lots of hassle and bargaining.

The biblical story of the 'loaves an fishes' comes to mind when it came to the feeding of the 'for hire operator'. It's hard to believe that you can have too much of a good thing, but such was the case when the woman of the house had her mind made up that you weren't going to die of starvation if she could help it. Maybe her mind set was still preparing grub for a thrashing gang for food was piled on your plate, and before you could wink a second helping was on its way. Refusal was tantamount to insult. Fortunately, farmer's wives are good cooks, but there was the odd exception. Entering a kitchen once, the smell of steak frying and spuds boiling was an aperitif for what was to come. The steak, smothered with spuds bursting from their jackets and piled high was placed before me. As I tucked in, the housewife, hovering anxiously between stove and table suddenly exclaimed,—"Oh god, I've given ye no gravy". She swept the pan off the stove and proceeded to pour the grease from the steak all over what was otherwise going to be a delicious meal. She saturated it, apologizing all the time for being so remiss. What does one do when faced with a soggy mess on your plate and the provider standing close by wishing to attend to your every wish? You eat it, and hope it doesn't come back up to give you a second bite at it! Another culinary story comes to mind when once baling hay for a neighbour. This man was unmarried and his housekeeper/mother was nearing her nineties. He being a bachelor and she being aged, I guess hygiene wasn't a high priority in the dairy end of housekeeping. White fleecy clouds moved before a brisk breeze and the sun beamed down; it was the ideal weather for baling. With two rounds of the field done and starting on the third himself appeared, carrying a cloth shopping bag (no plastic in those times) accompanied by a sheepdog. I throttled off and threw the clutch, the momentum of the machine slowly winding down. "A cup a tay to slake ye're thirst" was his greeting, handing me the shopping bag which contained a bottle of tea (cold) and some doorstep sandwiches. Kneeling down on a swath of hay I pulled the bottle from the bag removed the cork and took a swig; the taste of tea was mixed with the taste of sour milk The bachelor stood leaning against the baler, the dog settled himself down close by, his tail wagging and an expectant look on his face, I bit into one of the doorsteps and near choked. The taste and smell of rancid butter sent a message to my guts that made them churn. I held on. The dog moved closer; the speed of his wagging tail increased, and now it was my turn to move closer to the dog, for here was my ready-made refuse bin. We talked of this and that, mostly about the good drying conditions and I waited for the opportune moment. Eventually I made some inane comment about the hills being far away and what a good sign that was for continuing fine weather. The bachelor shifted his gaze to the far off hills and I threw the doorstep to the dog. He grabbed it in midair and almost immediately dropped it, took one sniff, then moved away a disgruntled look on his face. The rejected doorstep lay there on the ground for all to see and out of my reach. I shuffled and stretched and managed to throw a wisp of hay over it; the dog was hardly going to dig it up! Its comrade, still in the shopping bag, I craftily slipped into my shirt and dumped it when at the far end of the field. A concrete lined stomach would have been a big help when out for hire! These two stories are just a small sample of the vicissitudes that faced the 'for hire man' all those years ago when setting forth in his quest to make that few extra bob that would pay for the machine in no time!

Chapter 13
Neighbours

There is an old saying; "You can live without your relatives, but you can't live without your neighbours", and it hits the nail on the head no matter where you live, be it city or country. It probably applies more to rural parts, for relatively speaking, there is more isolation in rural living, and isolation breeds association, that, given a choice one might not necessary cultivate. Neighbours come in all sizes, classes, shapes and breeds, but I suppose the most important attribute to have is temperament. A sunny or surly disposition can make or mar a relationship between neighbours, especially if looking at one another over a broken down boundary fence! A pot-pouri of mankind, and its up to each individual to make a choice as to who he/she likes or dislikes, and then learn to live with him/her. Another old saying says, "If you want to know me come live with me". "Come live beside me" could equally apply. To learn to live with your neighbour in agreeable fashion is the objective, but not always attainable.

It would be incorrect to paint a picture of "everything's rosy" down on the farm. Unfortunately, there have been bitter feuds between neighbours, some going back generations, so long that the original reason for falling out has long been forgotten, but the old suspicions and real or imagined hurts still linger. We have all heard, and some of us can relate, stories of people being threatened or run off the land by some irate person slashook in hand, or of straying stock disappearing mysteriously, never to be seen again. A lot of these ancient feuds, aye, and some in more recent times, all started over nothing. A wrong word said or a word misunderstood in the heat of the moment.

We Irish have a propensity for delivering the verbal blow under the ribs, or below the belt on such occasions. We also have long memories! Intolerance over one's politics or religion, or plain begrudgery vis-à-vis size of farm are also possible reasons for coolness between neighbours, tho' not necessary downright feuding'. A very good example of this kind of animosity was portrayed in the play 'The Field' by that wonderful playwright J B Keane.

Fences and fencing are another cause of rows and rifts between neighbouring farmers. "Good Fences make Good Neighbours", was the title of a book written by Joseph Barber in 1958. It was about relations and relationships between Canada and the USA at the time, politics, business, and the people themselves. The same title could apply to farmers anywhere, where fences between them have to be maintained. A rough rule of thumb for boundary fences is that Farmer A maintains one half and Farmer B the other. Couldn't be simpler, except for the fact that boundary fences do not come in standard kit! They are made up in various shapes and sizes and could be described as an art form. Banks, ditches, hedges, straight post and wire, and very often a combination of all four. Who takes over what, and which end, is often a cause for *discussion,* and sometimes, downright argument. Getting that part sorted out, the next big step is the maintenance of same, and that's a continuous process. All animals, but especially sheep, seem to spend half their lives trying to break out into the neighbours land. Small, strong, wiry creatures, they seem to have a one track mind in their belief that the grass is always greener on the other side. There is no known reason for this behaviour, but there are a hundred reasons trotted out as to why it should be so. There're hungry? Bollocks, I've seen them up to their knees in grass yet push through to the neighbour's field that hasn't got a pick on it. They're looking for roughage? Rubbish, there's a rack of hay left out for them that they haven't touched. The wind has gone to the east? That's the best reason yet, for an east wind would unsettle yourself.

If there is any other animal designed to test the equanimity between neighbours, it surely must be the bulling heifer. Once she takes the notion into her head to go looking for a mate, it takes a lot of fence to stop her, and if she doesn't get satisfaction in the first field she enters, she'll keep travelling. Conversely, it a bullock breaks out to her, his mates'll follow him in jig time. The end result is: the boundary fence you thought was in good shape, now looks like the tank core had passed through it. The solution to that situation is straightforward. He /She who owns animals must keep them under control, but if there's any coolness between the parties involved it can cause some arge-bargee. "Dem bullocks ran da divil out'a me heifer, an hurt her hip". Stripped down to reality, what that statement means is—a few pounds (euros) compensation wouldn't go astray! A suitable reply, with money also in mind, could be as follows. "I had a man comin' to look at dem bullocks, but sure dey weren't fit to show. De lost a hundred (weight) chasing dat damn heifer". Check mate. Keeping control of your animals is a must for good relations between neighbours.

Believe it or not, but trees, beautiful an' all as they are, are very often a cause for dissension between neighbours, especially a large one growing on a boundary hedge. On one side of the hedge you have a tillage field; on the other side an' old pasture field. It's a source of irritation to the tillage farmer. It's large branches reaching out over his crop, causing lodging and maybe late ripening, that, and the fact that it's a great roosting place for crows who consider it a resting place between meals, having gorged themselves on his crop! He's all for cutting it down, or at least lopping off the boughs on his side, giving the tree a lopsided look The man on the other side isn't a bit worried about the tree. So what if the grass that grows under it is a bit rank, and not as edible as the rest of the field, its big spreading branches gives shade to his stock on a hot summers day, and gives a bit of shelter on a winters day. As far as he's concerned it looks good, adds beauty to the scene, and isn't doing' a bit aharm. Leave it there. Full stop. Another angle to the tree situation is where it's growing. If growing on the hedge part that is being maintained by the tillage man that gives him a bit of leverage, and visa-versa. Usually a comprise is reached in such situations, but there are times when King Solomon himself wouldn't settle it. It's that kind of problem that can get blown up out of all proportion, no one is satisfied, and ill feeling sets in.

An even worse situation can arise if a tree blows down, and to cap it all comes off an internal hedge running at right angles to the boundary hedge, but big enough for it's top to land out into the neighbours. Who claims the tree? I recall to mind just such an incident taking place many years ago between my father and the neighbour on our west side. Father dispatched two men forthwith, armed with crosscut and axe, (no chain saws if those days) to clear it off the neighbours land thinking he was doing the right thing. The neighbour, a bachelor, had different thinking. Hearing the rasp of a crosscut he went to investigate. A tall spare man, he bore down on the two lads in long swift strides. "What are yis at" he demanded, ignoring the obvious. "Clearin' da tops off for ya", was the reply. "Lave dem where de'ar, de'ar mine". Not wanting to get embroiled in an argument that wasn't of their making, they were only on a days pay, one of them set off to get the Boss-man, my father. He was sitting by the fire with his boots off taking an afternoon nap, (a bit under the weather from a heavy cold) and his health wasn't improved by the news that was taking place down the fields. Pulling his boots on, he too set off in long swift strides.

"What's tha' matter wid ya", was his opening remark.

"Dem is my sticks, dere in my field"

"They're off my tree", came the sharp reply. "Ar'nt we tidyin' dem off the field for ya"

"I didn't axed ya to" was the rejoinder.

The battle of words continued in a tit for tat fashion, then came the 'dig in the ribs' throw away remark.

"Yis want everythin'."

"I don't want notin' ya can have da damned sticks".

"Yis can keep yer damned kippeens, I'll be warm without dem."

That was the final remark from the neighbour as he turned and stormed away.

"Yer a contrary ould bachelor", was the last final shout from Father.

His orders to the two lads was to throw the few lengths they had cut back over his side, and to cut the rest off at the exact spot where the tree lay on the boundary and leave the rest. And there they lay and rotted away, for neither wanted them at this stage. Two contrary stubborn men, not willing to give in, in the heat of the moment, but neither were they going to fall out. They had always respected and supported one another, and that way they remained till the Lord himself called them.

There is a special kind of neighbour in every parish, one that comes in for a lot of stick and sarcastic comment from all the others, not in his hearing of course. The "Know All". Well up in all aspects of agriculture, especially the ones he's not involved in, he will pass judgement on every topic, and will hold forth down in his local or at the meeting after the meeting (pub gathering) and tell how it should be done. Blind everyone with science he will, and gladly give a progress report on how he's doing on his place. His percentages and yields are a mite above national average and certainly above those living around him! He always it seems, gets to sell before the bottom falls out of the market. His animals always make top grade, and his yields per acre are second to none. Gets his crop off when everyone else is struggling with the weather. In other words a good farmer who manages to raise the ire of those who have to listen to him.

The Know All we had in our parish always took the wife on an expensive holiday at a time when the average farmer's idea of a holiday was a day at the races. This didn't pass unnoticed by the wives of his neighbours who dropped hints about taking a weekend somewhere before the summer was out. The reply to such hints were always short, and expressed with some malice.

"Sure he can well afford it, doesn't everyone know his ould grandmother owned a brewery and left him loaded." Depending on the ire and bile of the moment this 'brewery' could be a Scotch distillery, or potin making in the wilds of Connamara, and she in her bare feet at that.

I call to mind a neighbour who paid her yearly Xmas visit to distant cousins; two bachelors in their fifties and ruled over by a domineering mother. Enquiring solicitously as to their welfare she asked one of them. "How are you, cousin Charlie"? "Not bad, at all at all, but ya know what, I could do with a bit iv a holiday." "Holiday," harrumphed the mother garrulously, "weren't ye down in Lisdoonvarna a while back" conveniently forgetting that that wild weekend to Lisdoonvarna had taken place a couple of years ago. Lisdoonvara in County Clare and Courtown Harbour on the east coast are well known 'watering holes' for rural folk.

However we all have our pitfalls and slip-ups from time to time and Mr Know All was no exception. An innocent remark is usually enough information to build a story on! Down at the grain plant one harvest the young lad at the intake point let slip; "So and So had a load rejected yesterday." The recipient of this marvellous piece of gossip couldn't wait to pass it on, and savoured the moment down in the pub one night.

"Hey lads, ya know what?"

"No, we don't know what, tell us".

"Yer man had a load downed 'ere yesterday".

"Go on, who t'ould ya".

"The young lad takin' it in, all sprouted it was, and 30% moisture, t'would hardly tip outa da trailer".

"Cripes, dat bates all".

"Jasus, couldn't a happened to a nicer fella".

"Some bollocks," put a finish to the conversation.

In county living and probably in cities too, its other's misfortunes mixed in with your own that helps keep a balance in life, and gossiping about them helps pass the time of a long winter's night.

There's no doubt about it, but when help is needed or trouble looms, the real worth of good neighbours comes into play. The following tale relates to the generosity and helpfulness of good neighbours regardless of the hour called upon. The central figure was a young bride right out of the heart of the city, my wife! She was totally new and unaware to country life, and all its manifestations. She settled in smartly, and was determined, (the country in-laws would be keeping a close eye), not only to run a good house, but to learn all about farming and where she could best be of assistance. We were married in the Fall of the year and with the initials SRN, SCM, after her name she eagerly awaited Springtime. Springtime was lambing time, and here surely she could show off her prowess should any maternity problems arise! Long before the first lamb was dropped she had made her preparations. Sterilised needles and syringe, bottle of penicillin, and clean white sheet. Farmers, she had noted to herself, were no prize winners when it came to hygiene, and hygiene was one of the first principles of the maternity ward.

The first lambs came mid February, and so did a black east wind, and sooner than expected she had her first case. I had got an invitation to a wedding stag party and she almost pushed me out the door in her eagerness to take charge. I did a last minute check on the flock and satisfied that all was OK took off. An aged aunt from nearby had come in to baby-sit the young bride, for she was still a bit fearful of the emptiness of the countryside, especially at night. The aunt, of farming stock had no fear of anything, and eagerly looked forward to participating in any action that might arise.

Round about midnight the pair set off in an uncovered ancient Willy's jeep, to take a last check before turning in, the sheepdog sitting between them. He probably knew more about the job than the pair of them put together. Circling slowly, the headlamps sweeping the field all seemed quiet, then they spotted her. A lone cheviot ewe away from all the others, and tucked in close to a stonewall sheltering from the bitter wind. As the jeep approached she jumped up. Dazzled by the headlamps and the sight of two muffled up figures bearing down on her spooked her completely. She took off. However, both shepherds noted a lambs head protruding from her rear end.

The first step in taking a lamb from a ewe is similar to making hare soup. First catch your animal. Out in the middle of a thirty acre field it's an almost impossible job, especially if the subject is a hardy two year old cheviot. The dog eventually took charge. Hopping out of the jeep he headed her, and fixing her with his hypnotic stare he backed her to the wall. The bride pounced. Hanging on for all she was worth she eventually got the ewe under control, and with auntie sitting on her head, she set to at the other end. Try as she might she couldn't shift that lamb, and saying, "Come on Missus push harder" was to no avail, for Missus didn't understand a word she said! She wasn't to know, till many births later, that a lamb delivery is somewhat different than a human baby. Time was passing, the ewe was getting tired, and the lamb wouldn't live if left much longer. The bride was now desperate, how could she face her husband with a dead lamb, and maybe a dead ewe, and she so full of confidence only a few short hours ago. "You may go for help", suggested auntie, whose enthusiasm was not so vibrant as it had been a few hours ago. The black east wind blowing around and up her skirt, (she didn't approve of women wearing slacks) had killed off all desire to be helpful. She was past seventy and it was past 1am. Swallowing her pride, the bride climbed into the jeep and drove to the nearest neighbours, two bachelor brothers. The noise of the engine awoke the brothers; one of them stuck his head out the upstairs window.

"Who's dere" he demanded.

Filled with confusion and apologies, she blurted out her troubles. She was almost in tears.

"G'wan back, we'll be wit ye in a minute, whare are yis?".

"Top of the lawn, by the wall".

"OK".

In no time flat the brothers arrived and took charge.

"G'wan down now da pair a ye an put da kettle on an make a mug a tay for us all," instructed the taller of the two, "an we'll be down aftar ye in no time."

The young bride was somewhat taken aback by the order. She felt she should be there, if for no other reason then to see where she'd gone wrong. And with the husband away, was she not in charge? Did they not realise that she was an SRN, SCM, and until her marriage of a few short months ago this sort of situation was commonplace to her. Her feminine ire rose briefly, then, subsided. Routing neighbours out of bed in the small hours of the morning and a black frost blowing doesn't leave much room for argument. A fleeting moment of awkwardness passed between all four, then the penny dropped with the bride.

Shyness was preventing these two rugged countrymen from getting on with the business of attending to the ewe. It's hard to credit, in this secular, and dare I say promiscuous age that we live in today, that that was the reason, but it was so. Their sensitivities would not allow them to handle a female, albeit a ewe, in front of other females. Pride swallowed and the message taken, the two ladies climbed onto the jeep and headed for the kitchen. The hygienic white sheet, stiff with frost and now the colour of grass was fired into the back, there to become a sleeping bag for the dog! The tay was barely wet, before the two men arrived at the back door. "Dere'ye are Missus, a fine pair a twins she have, an neary a bother on dem, an she's in da sheltar a da wall outa da wind." Had she known them a bit better the bride would have hugged and kissed them? They all sat down to tay and sandwiches, and the bride still feeling that she hadn't shown enough gratitude, popped a pie in the oven. It was one she had made with tender loving care for the husband, but he could wait. The lot was swept. Bachelors don't refuse grub, and with full bellies and heat from the stove everyone was in right good humour. Sleep was gone, the adrenaline from success still flowing. When the husband (me) arrived home it seemed he had left one party to arrive at another. Both were parties of goodwill, but the one in the farm kitchen cemented a friendship that was never broken.

By and large, and over time most all neighbours get along. It's hard enough fighting the elements, and there's plenty to occupy your time, so squabbling with the person next door is mostly wasted effort. The mechanisation of farming, especially the two big ones haying and harvesting, has reduced the labour force to a one or two man job. Good for progress, bad for co-operative effort. The meithal (gathering of helpers) has practically disappeared, and mores the pity. Countless stories can be told of neighbour support and help in the rural areas. On a one to one basis, and in spite of progress, rural neighbours still stand foursquare behind one another. You won't ever see "By Appointment Only" nailed to a farmhouse door.

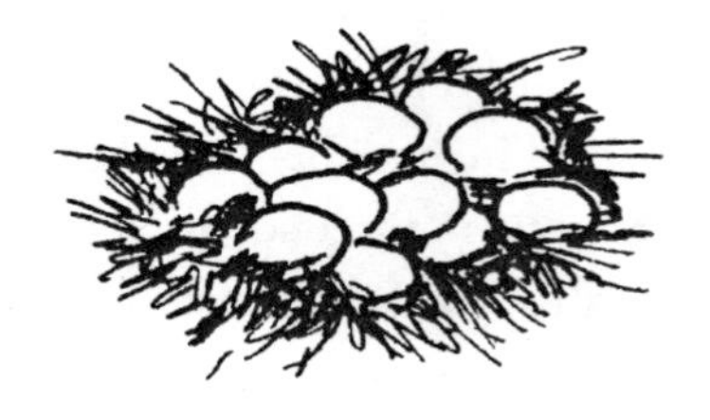

Chapter 14
A Settin' of Eggs

With the 'war effort' over and manufacturers anxious to turn their swords into ploughshares tractors became more freely available, soon taking over from the horse all the heavy work on farms such as field cultivations and ploughing. However, there was one area where progress remained slow, and that was in and around the farmyard. A farm the size of ours always had a yardman, milkman, or herd. Any of the three names would fit the job, but from the social ladder point of view there was a mite difference. On a very big place (demesne or estate) herd would be the acceptable name. On our place he carried the name yardman. This man had a certain status in the worker hieratical system. He only joined the field workers when all yard chores were completed, and in the winter when animals were housed and fed indoors his was a full time job and required a helper at times. On our farm there was a big turn over in yardmen. I don't remember the reason for this, but I suspect maybe that there wasn't enough space between my Father and the various men who took up the position!! They came from far and near. The ones from far away 'lived in', in other words they got board and lodging. My Mother fed them three square meals a day and they slept in a room in the yard. Bedding was provided.

The farmyard was a busy place during the winter months. Stall fed cattle tied up by the neck had food fed to them twice a day. Cows, calves, workhorses and pigs, also got the same treatment. Turnips hauled in from the field and tipped up, fresh straw for bedding hauled from the rick in the haggard, and the waste (dung) hauled out. This was where the helper came in.

In the middle of all this activity was the humble hen. She was probably well down the social ladder in the farm animal hierarchy, nevertheless her contribution to the food chain was not inconsiderable. The few hens scratching 'round the farmyard are fast disappearing on Irish farms today, yet it was a common enough sight in my young days. High production, quick turnover, out of the shell and into the pot in five weeks is the theme now-a- days. The laying hen now confined to a battery cage. Just like the pig, the ultimate in factory farming. Mind you, with people getting more conscious of their eating habits and what they eat, the demand for organic foods is increasing, so maybe the lowly hen will find herself back in the farmyard and back in demand for her free range eggs and become a sort of status symbol on any farm. As I've already said she wasn't high in the farmyard pecking order, nevertheless she paid her way in keeping the house in eggs and meat and when on full lay was able to keep the farmers wife in pin money from the sale of surplus eggs.

In springtime, a young man's fancy turns to thoughts of love, and so it is with the barnyard rooster who stepped around struttin' his stuff and crowing vaingloriously, hens go off the lay and become broody. This springtime madness created a problem for all farmers' wives, Mother included, for the broody hen was a crafty one when it came to plotting and planning where she would lay and hatch her eggs. She would burst out of the henhouse in the morning with all the others when Mother threw them a scatterin' of oats in the yard. A peck here a peck there she would slowly separate herself from the bunch and in zig - zag fashion go a-searching in a nonchalant fashion. It's hard to visualise a nonchalant hen! Everyone was alerted to the situation. "Anyone seen that speckled hen?" "I seen her headin' for the back haggard, Mam." We kids were always roped in (t'would keep us out of mischief) and we hated it, for a bunch of nettles or high briers was always a choice spot of the broody hen. We would go about looking and poking with a length of stick, lifting briers and beating down nettles, getting stung and scratched for our efforts If, or when found, there were two options. Leave her there and let her hatch out, and hope the fox didn't get her. The second option was to catch her and put her in a hen-coop on her own, hoping that the move didn't put her off the idea. Hens like humans have varying temperaments. The good mother hen clucked away and made fussing noises when you slipped a hand in under her to check on how things were going. The bad tempered one squawked and flapped and if not careful you got a sharp peck on the hand. If the clocker managed to avoid the search party there was always great excitement, when twenty odd days later she arrived in the yard with her brood of yellow chicks. Cluck, Cluck, Cluck, breaking up morsels of food with her beak and dropping them for her young. They, making a wild dash for the shredded morsel, squabbling and fighting amongst themselves for the best pieces. Weary Willie on the outside of the circle cheep cheep cheeping away hoping mother or someone would listen to his tale of woe. He often snuffed it, for the survival of the fittest just like the jungle is farmyard law.

To change the bloodline and improve the flock Mother often got a settin' of eggs elsewhere. There was always someone in the parish well known for having a good line. Once again, some member of the younger generation would be dispatched (no phones) to enquire if Mrs So&So would "Keep me a settin' a eggs." "Ask her how much, an' when wou'tha be ready, I have a hen on the cluck." The price would be humble enough, a few bob.(shillings) but could entail a bit of bargaining, or maybe a barter scheme would go through. A couple of jars of fruit, preserved from the previous autumn in kilner jars, in exchange. I should mention that not all eggs were hatched or sold or eaten, some were preserved in a solution of waterglass, (silicate of soda, ten parts to a hundred of water.) and mainly used for baking.

I mentioned previously that my Father would overlook any 'light fingered' foibles a man might have, so long as he was a good worker. However, there was a limit to such practices, and if stuff moving off the place became patently obvious he took steps to correct matters. Taking such things as eggs, spuds, or a turnip or two to help feed a large family was OK, but lifting product for resale was a horse of a different colour, especially if the man under suspicion was single! On one such occasion the items disappearing were eggs, and for the man concerned it was a poor choice, for he was dipping into the housewife's pin money, in this case my Mothers. It was the time of year when the hens were at full stretch (no pun intended) producing eggs to beat the band.

Mother it was who brought it to his attention that the hens had gone 'off lay' This was not unusual, for hens are daft creatures; any little upset such as a fox or even a farm dog paying them too much attention can throw their laying pattern out of sync. Normally, hens and their laying pattern wouldn't have been high on my Fathers list of priorities, but when Mother complained of loss of income he sat up and took notice.

"I don't know what's the matter" she complained, "They're young hens, I'm feeding them same as always." Father decided to do a bit of sleuthing. He 'bided his time and kept a careful watch. No results. Then, the first clue came on the grapevine. Apparently the local shopkeeper in the nearby village was doing a roaring trade in eggs These eggs were talked about in glowing terms, big, and lovely orange yellow yolks. Demand far exceeded supply in spite of above average price per dozen. Down in the shop one day getting himself some tobacco he and the shopkeeper gossiped about the weather and this and that. Casually, he asked for a dozen of them good eggs, muttering something about been a bit short at home. The shopkeeper replied he had none in stock at the moment, but would be getting some later on that evening. Clue number two. Father reckoned that most deliveries to shops were during opening hours, if these eggs were coming in the evening it had to be a back door job. He pocketed his tobacco and left, satisfied that it was his eggs that were the talk of the town. He would have liked to ask who the supplier was, but he knew he'd be pushing his luck. The shopkeeper was a taciturn sort of fella, didn't ask anyone any questions, neither did he offer any unnecessary answers! If perchance the eggs were hot, he had no intention of handing my Father a rope to make a noose for his own neck.

Fathers next move was to do a search of the farmyard

buildings, having sent the suspect to do some fencing at the furthest end of the land. Turning over an old roofing sheet that was laying along a wall in one of the outhouses he found what he was looking for, a dozen or so of shiny, fresh laid eggs, and not laid there by a hen. He hid himself on a loft that evening and watched the suspect spirit them away just before quitting time. The Book of Evidence complete the next step was confrontation, and that caused Father a problem. He was a firm believer in the old saying, "Better the devil you know, than the devil you don't know." The suspect was a good worker and Father had no objection to the odd egg going the wrong way, but this was wholesale larceny. He scratched his head and did some serious thinking. To confront the fella was going to lead to a stand up row and dismissal and that he wished to avoid. Like any good detective working on a case he badly needed a break, and it came in a most unusual fashion. He was out one day slashing nettles with a slashook and came across a deserted hens nest. She had either been frightened, or gone off the hatch. He picked one egg up and holding it close to his ear shook it. Glug, glug, as rotten as rotten could be. Kneeling down he carefully placed them in his cap, a wolfish grin on his face. He had the answer to his problem. At an opportune moment he switched them with the shiny fresh ones stashed behind the roofing sheet, then sat back and awaited the grapevine news! It wasn't long in coming. "Eggs shot off the pan, the gue hitting the ceiling" was one report.

Children coughing an' spluttering as if they had the croup, as the sulphurous fumes wafted out of the kitchen and percolated through the house. Husbands gone to work on empty bellies exiting their homes like the Exodus from Egypt In spite of inclement weather all doors and windows were left open to clear the houses of the nauseous stench. Irate housewives laid siege to the shop and told the owner in articulate but impolite language where he could stuff his eggs. He in turn, and in even more direct language told his supplier where he could go, and bring all his relations with him, if he had any!

One night, a week or so later Mother remarked that the hens were laying to beat the band and wondering if she should preserve or sell the surplus. He advised her to preserve them, as there wasn't a great demand locally just at present and prices would be poor. Laying down his pipe he headed for bed, "Just take a bit a time, an' things will work out", were his last thoughts before he dozed off.

Chapter 15
Pin Money

To day we see and hear a lot about equality for women. Watch the T V, read a daily paper, its all there. Equality in golf and tennis clubs, equality in the work and market place, not forgetting equality in the home, but the one that makes the most news is equality in the pay packet, be it factory floor or corporate office. Women, and their subsequent inequalities in the work force is not a new phenomena, it's just more highlighted today, and grabs a lot of attention in the local, national, and betimes international news. Like a pot simmering away on the edge of a stove, these inequalities have been bubbling away for years, eventually boiling over by the arrival of the suffragettes, and Emily Parkhurst chaining herself to those railings in London. That was the start I guess, and since that time women and their rights have come a long way, with representation on their behalf coming from various quarters, notably their trade unions. However, most of the benefits have accrued to women in mass occupations, mills, factories, offices, and the professions, leaving out on a limb the farm wife.

To day we don't give a second thought to the young farmer's wife holding down a permanent job, be it nursing, physiotherapy, solicitor, or what have you. In some cases, if the farm is small it's a financial necessity. As recent as forty or fifty years ago such was not the case, and the farmer's wife was very much confined behind the farm gate Was the farmer so well off, that he could afford to keep his wife at home, and in the lap of luxury? I don't think so. Times were different, and the farms more self sufficient, but self sufficiency doesn't fall out of the sky. It takes a lot of hard work to create it and sustain it.

The farm dwelling alone was a real boiler house! Few, if any, electrical gadgets in some houses, no electricity, so the scrubbing, rubbing, shining and polishing was done by the sweat of ones' brow. Throw in a few yard chores like feeding a couple of calves or pigs, minding a pet lamb or two, and keeping an eye on the vegetable garden was a pretty permanent job, that and raising a family!

I don't know where the term "Pin Money" originated from, but I'm sure it applies to all persons urban or rural who manage successfully to siphon off some monies, usually small, from either a regular pay packet or from goods or services sold, and use it for extra necessaries; birthdays, family and Xmas presents, or a small luxury or two. In the hungry thirties farm produce such as eggs and butter were traded for items such as tea and sugar, and if there was any surplus cash it wouldn't buy much more then a packet of pins. Maybe that's the answer. The rearing and selling of turkeys was a big one for the farmer's wife, and if she had a hand in the rearing of calves, pigs, or pet lambs, the price of one of them usually came her way. Most of that windfall would be ploughed back into the household and anything left over could be classed as "Pin Money".

Financially speaking the first big break through for the farm wife, provided she wished to avail of it, was the decision of Bord Failte (the Tourist Board) to encourage farm holidays for the tourists who were coming into the country in increasing numbers. Pin Money turned into real money. The folding stuff, in the form of fivers and tenners were pressed into her hand, as she waved one set of tourists away and then into the bedroom to tear the sheets off the bed and get it ready for more coming in that evening.

In today's terms the money was small enough : £4 / £5 Bed and Breakfast, evening meal £2 / £3, but it was coming in every day from Easter through to Sept / Oct, and the price of a calf or pig once a year was penny ante stuff in comparison. To do up the house, buy a labour saving gadget or two for the kitchen, put a down payment on your own car, but most important of all, was to be financially independent. T'was heady stuff. The work was hard and constant, but stuffing those green backs into your purse helped lighten the load.

Up at 6am, preparing hearty breakfasts, baking soda and brown bread, changing bed linen and washing same, and keeping the place spick and span didn't leave any idle moments. To get started one had to adhere to the strict rules and regulations as laid down by Bord Failte, but when you hung their seal of approval on your gate, and the local tourist office had your phone number you were in business. Money wasn't the only advantage; to sit in your own sitting room and talk to people from all over the globe and from all walks of life was something else. Learning about other cultures, hearing how other folk lived, and swapping ideas was an education in itself, and also gave you the chance to act as ambassador without portfolio for your own country.

Now a days farm holidays are an accepted form of leisure, and the trials and errors of start up have been ironed out, but for those who got in on the ground floor there were a few hick ups and not a few funny incidences. There was the case of the girl in the tourist office who booked a city couple onto a farm a few miles away. An hour later the couple were back at the office saying the bulls wouldn't let them drive down the avenue to the farmhouse. The farm entrance had a cattle grid and a bunch of ordinary bullocks were standing at it when the couple arrived. In spite of being in the safety of their car they were fearful of driving through a bunch of docile bullocks. The girl at the office assuring them that all was O K, and that the farm would hardly hang out a sign saying "visitors welcome," and then threaten them with wild bulls was to no avail. They wished to be booked into a nice quiet town house. Farm life as viewed from the other side!

Then there was the house that had three couples staying at one and the same time. One pair from France, one from Germany, and the last pair from England. A good cross- section of foreign visitors enjoying farm holidays. The first two pair spent their time sight seeing; the last pair were attending a three day horse event nearby. He was an ex tank commander from World War 2, and looked old enough to have done a stint in World War 1. She was younger and a good deal prettier! They drove a snappy sports car, which the Commander let all and sundry know was the wife's run around, at home, he drove a Daimler

The third day of the horse event poured out of the heavens as only an Irish day can, and the pair came in on the late side and very miserable looking. The others were seated in the dining room starting their evening meal. The host, feeling sorry for the old Commander and with generosity of spirit poured him a large "Crested Ten" (whiskey) which he downed in one gulp. The host topped up the glass.

The first glass thawed him out; the second one loosened his tongue. Starting with the dastardly weather, the poor performance of the horses, a quick resume of the Daimler's qualities (it seemed Arctic weather or a wet Irish day would have no check on it's performance), he then proceeded to give us a blow by blow account of the "Rout of Rommel" and the whole North African Campaign. Every so often in the saga he would interject with the words, "By Gad Sir, we gave the Boche a thrashing," thumping the sideboard with his fist. The host became alarmed. Sitting not ten feet away were the German couple. Their English wasn't great, and that worried him. The Commander kept using the "royal we," but would they, understand? And the French didn't always side with the English when trouble broke out! He had no intention of insulting any of his guests, they were paying good money to stay under his roof, neither did he want to be at the centre of World War 3, if it broke out. What would the wife say: she'd give him some stick should any of the guests leave in high dudgeon? His first thoughts were to pour the Commander a third glass. It might make him slur his speech and be not so distinct, or vocal. But he looked like a man who could knock off a whole bottle and stay marching, or talking. It was the wife who saved the situation, by placing before the Commander a steaming hot plate of Irish stew with lashings of mashed potatoes, and the promise of apple pie with cream to follow, and in an aside to the host asked if there might be a drop of brandy for all when the meal was over, it been such a miserable cold damp evening! She held out the chair for him and he sat down, beaming benignly at all in the room, and set forth to do battle with the mountain of grub on his plate. After dinner he settled himself in an armchair and the snores emanating from him sounded like shells from a tank, obviously the "Rout of Rommel" was being replayed.

Its changed days and changed ways since the original "Pin Money" was so assiduously hoarded and saved for the rainy day or special gift. If today a farmer's wife was seen walking down the street of any rural town with a basket of eggs and butter on her arm, it would be thought, that she was on some film set. She would also run the risk of being arrested for peddling foodstuffs, no not drugs, foodstuffs, for she would be in breach of some piddling E C directive. As the man said "That's progress."

Chapter 16
Daisy the House Cow

Before leaving the farmyard the House Cow is worth a mention. Not like the humble hen, who rated low on the social scale, Daisy the house cow was high up on the farmyard priorities list. Today's modern dairy herd like the broiler chicken or pig fattening unit has more or less replaced the house cow. Herring bone parlours, circular parlours, easy feed and self feed is a far cry from Daisy's day, who, apart from the farmer's wife, was probably the most important female on any farm regardless of its size. A good house cow was held in high esteem for she was the anchor pin to other projects on the farm. If she got sick or went dry other enterprises suffered accordingly.

The number of cows kept on any farm then or now is related to farm size. Some supplied milk to the local creamery, others to the liquid mild trade, but Daisy was distinct from the commercial herd. Her first priority was to keep the house in milk and butter, the skim milk went to feed a calf or maybe a couple of bons (young pigs), the hens got a drop, and of course the yard cats and farm dog. So all in all her welfare was important to other creatures on the farm plus the farmer, for the bons and calf were eventually turned into money, the hens kept laying with surplus eggs sold and the yard cats kept the rats and mice down. Daisy herself, at the top of her lactation provided surplus butter for sale. Today's TV ads tell us that milk is the perfect food, and there's no doubt but a quick glance at any of the abovementioned animals on any farm could tell you if Daisy was on top of her job. The calf would have a gloss on his pelt, the pigs a shine in their hair, and the cat's hair smooth and silky.

Our farm was no different than any other of its time. We usually had two cows in milk with a third either drying up or springing (close to calving). During busy times, when all hands were fully occupied either haying or harvesting, it was left to us kids to bring in Daisy and her followers for evening milking, and when we got 'hardy' were expected to get on with the milking. If Daisy deserved this exalted position of queen of the farmyard it was only in her head, for we kids had a different opinion! Daisy is a pretty common name for the said queen in this country, but in other countries she is called Bossy and it is an apt name, for manys the milkman or maid and that includes us kids, stood at the yard gate calling "Ho Bossy, Ho Bossy" while Bossy tugged away at a patch of succulent grass at the far end of the field maybe lifting her head once to let you know she'd heard but only ready to come in her own good time. If fact the only reason she headed for the yard gate was the pressure of milk building up in a tight udder, or if the weather was inclement and she wanted in out of the elements to face into a rack of hay.

It wasn't the done thing to chase a milch cow with a dog, but in exasperation we kids, especially if only one of us was detailed to get in Daisy/Bossy would encourage Shep (most farm dogs got stuck with that bloody awful name) to lend a hand. Shep wasn't stupid and knew from experience that cows could be very contraire females and not to be tangled with at close range. He would circle out wide, then, come up from behind giving out a threatening bark. Daisy would take note of the manoeuvre give a toss of her head and go on grazing. Sheps' next move was to dart in and give her a good nip on the hock. He had to be quick; otherwise he got sore ribs for himself, for Daisy was deft with either hind leg. A nip was enough to get her moving, but at her pace. Ambling along she would frequently stop to pull a wad of grass for herself, just to let Shep know it was she who was dictating the speed limit.

Boss or Queen of her own domain she certainly was. Coming from or going to the farmyard she would have a retinue of followers, another cow, a weanling or two, a couple of young heifers. She would pace along at her own gait, tossing her head at any of the followers who might be tempted to move ahead of her, and should one feel frisky enough to get out of line and run right ahead she would charge at them snorting through her nose and give them a good puck for their audacity. Once into the yard she would head for the cow house, line up in her stall stick her nose into the trough or hayrack to see what was available. If nothing was there she sometimes did a quick U- turn and out into the yard again to let you know she was displeased.

"Variations on a thyme" is a piece of music. It could easily apply to the many variations of Daisies that lived on farms. Big ones, small ones, purebreds, crossbreds, even tempered ones, cross tempered ones, even the best of them had mood swings.

How was Daisy chosen in the first place? Well there was no hard or fast rule, but when you got a good one you held on to her till her teeth fell out. One could be purchased at the local fair either springing down (due to calve soon) or freshly calved, or purchased from a neighbour.

Farm kids got an early introduction as to how life got started; the process of procreation. Not for them the hoary old tale or myth of been born under a cabbage leaf. Even when an attempt was made to hide the facts of life coincidence often blew the cover. A classic example: a ewe might have yeaned or a cow calved, and one of the children (usually the eldest) would be dispatched to check if mother and offspring were OK. A peep over the door was all was needed, but that quick peep sometimes revealed a mine of information, for there lay Daisy or ewe, pushing out a brother or sister to the first born. That quick peep was as good as a lecture in maternity. The other end of the conundrum was solved when Daisy's once a year day of pleasure took place. "Takin' the cow to the bull", was often the excuse offered up to the teacher by a young lad on missing a day at school! Incidentally, this superior knowledge was used mercilessly by us farm yokels when visited by our city cousins, (townies). Full of knowledge about the 'latest show in town' they would feign mild surprise that we hadn't seen it, or even know about it, but what goes round comes round and when we got our innings we made the most of it. We played it two ways; with knowing nods an' smirks between us, we kept them in suspense or second guessing. The second method was to feed them all the gory details of giving birth; blood, afterbirth, the lot, was trotted out, but the greatest titillation was achieved by an in depth account of the 'visit to the bull'. All the action was explained in great detail. Looks of horror, looks of disbelief, (you're having us on) and looks of sheer sensual pleasure, appeared on their faces. Another big excitement was milking time, when city kids were on a visit or holiday. Urged on by the country cousins to have a go they'd pull and squeeze on Daisy's tits, all to no avail. Daisy patiently would move from leg to leg, giving the odd switch of her tail and wonder what the hell was going on. Then we would step in 'an' show 'em' how it was done. The milk going into the pail "pish-wish pish wish," the froth coming up over the side of the bucket, Daisy at her ease chewing the cud, and giving the odd digestive burp.

Daisy's day out often caused havoc, not only on her place of residence, but all other farms on her way to her suitor, for a Daisy feeling her oats was a formidable female. On that day, she was neither proud nor particular, and on the way if the occasion arose she could switch to lesbian, or transvestite, and back to tantalising female. This is where the Young Lad came in. In our particular case the bull was only down the road and yours truly would be sent on in front to close gates along the way, and stand in gaps where the fencing was poor (a common enough feature). The man in charge of operations, the yardman, would bring up the rear. Our work was cut out for Daisy always moved along at a jog trot. Animals in adjoining fields caught the scent and jogged along with her inside the fence. At any moment Daisy would do a Houdini through a thorn hedge or wire fence leading the animals she had joined a merry chase. Getting her back on track was a major chore. The big moment she had waited for was over in a jump, and she was on her way home a lot more manageable, tiredness had overcome frenzied passion!

Twice a day seven days a week the round of the year, she plodded in and out of her milking stall. Summer or winter was all the same to her, but for the milker the seasonal change had its consequences. Summer time brought flies, and they were a constant irritant to Daisy. Switching her tail across her back continually to brush them off, she often lashed it across the milker's neck and ears. The grass being lush and her dung being soft, he or she didn't leave the milking shed smelling of roses!

Daisy's factory parts come in various shapes and sizes and could be a bother for the hand milker. The correct terminology is udder and teat, but down on the farm are known as bag or elder, tits or spins. One talks of a cow as having a good bag under her, or maybe light in one spin, caused by a touch of mastitis, the bane of all cows and owners. One with a bottle elder or very short tits was the worst of all cases. In the first instance, one needed massively long fingers to get around the tits, the second case was a finger and thumb exercise.

Some times, a hand picked Daisy turned out to be a big disappointment, for in spite of her shape, size, or colour, she was a kicker. In spite of all efforts to control this habit she'd kick the sun moon and stars, and many a new milking pail was turned into a piece of crumpled metal before it got run in. She was sold forthwith; let someone else train her. Even the best of them had a crass streak, and for no known reasons only to themselves, would let fly with a hind leg and over would go pail, stool, and milker. The only pleased ones were the cats, chasing all over the cow house lapping up the rivulets of milk that were flowing in all directions. Milking was not a male preserve, and it was often said that women milkers were better than men. Probably more gentle and patient; a better understanding of their female counterpart.

The arrival of the small portable milking machine was the first step in mechanising the cow house. Today's milking parlour looks like a hospital operating theatre, milk moving from cow to cooler through tubes and pipes untouched by human hand. Wall to wall tiling and the milk person (horrible word that) dressed like a nurse of surgeon. Progress? Must be. Daisy couldn't care less she'll still amble in and out, twice a day seven days a week, with a short maternity leave.

Chapter 17
Sheep

Specialised farming is in vogue nowadays but in my young days mixed farming applied on nearly all farms big and small. It was a mixed blessing. The advantages were obvious. If one crop or project didn't come up to expectations in any given year something else took up the slack. It was usually in the form of an unexpected price rise due to market fluctuations beyond the farmers control, nevertheless, if someone hit the jackpot either by design or fluke, he was considered a 'smart operator'. Too many irons in the fire was the downside to a mixed operation. Come the 'fine day', and a farmer could find himself going in several directions all at the same time! Roots to be thinned, hay to be cut, sheep to be shorn, the divil an'all to be done and clouds gathering on the horizon. And that brings me to another farm animal that doesn't qualify for any citation in my book, but nevertheless must get a mention. Of all the cussed contrary animals that ever drew breath, sheep must come near the top of the league.

Sheep have been part of the Irish farming scene since forever I suppose. They too have benefited from the over all progress that has been achieved in agriculture during the later half of the twentieth century. But the benefits have been mostly on the side of the sheep and not on the owners or handlers. New and improved worm and fluke doses. Better sheep dips for the control of that summer scourge, the maggot. Winter housing for the pregnant ladies. Nice new low loading stock trailers with low ramps for easy entry and exit. No jumping from a height of three of four feet landing on your knees, and the followers from behind jumping on top of you. New penning and handling facilities, on the farms and at livestock marts. No doubt about it sheep have it made, for the benefits and improvements have been mostly on their side, but the handling of them still uses up a lot of sweat and effort.

And speaking of sweat and effort I recall my first introduction to shearing. A young lad of my age had come to work for us. His credentials were impeccable for his father had been working on the farm for most of his life, and his mother helped my mother at spring cleaning and other busy times in the house. He started his apprenticeship as a sort of general factotum or dogs body; digging garden spuds for the dinner, hauling spring water from the well for my mother on butter making days, keeping logs into the fire in winter, a general roust-a-bout. We were at an age when testosterone levels were running high in both of us, and we were fit for anything; couldn't wait to be at 'mans work'! God help our innocence.

Father had purchased a score of cast ewes in late spring.

The idea was to fatten them up then sell. A quick turnover, a quick buck to be earned before the first of the lambs became fit. So far so good. The first thing to be done was shear them, for a shorn ewe fattens faster than one carrying her fleece; that was the perceived wisdom. He normally got in a professional Shearer for the main flock, but figured he'd be wasting the man's time just to come and shear twenty. At least that's what he told us pair of eager beavers. What he didn't tell us was that the ewes had a touch of mange and that was the reason he had got them cheap from some dealer who had literally pulled the wool over Father's eyes. It was illegal and still is to move sheep with mange. The guy had pulled a fast one. Realising his mistake too late there was nothing for it but to shear, dip, and hope; mange is hard to kill. To tell the truth he hadn't the effrontery to get in the professional who very likely would spread the gossip all over the parish leaving Father with egg on his face!

We set too with a will on a cold May day with a hand shears each, (electric or motor powered clippers were not yet on the market.), determined to out shear each other. The coolness of the weather also played a significant part on our operation for the yolk (grease) of the sheep's wool is slow to rise in cold weather. Sitting tight on the skin, and coupled with a touch of mange and poor body condition made for tough shearing. Today's professionals can knock a fleece off in about seventy seconds; it took us the best part of a day and some of the next to complete the job. Cursing, sweating, heaving and wrestling, somehow or other we managed to haul the fleeces off them. Naturally the ewes didn't take too kindly to being mismanaged, they joined in the wrestling with gusto giving back all that was handed out to them in spades! Sitting chatting some days later and discussing what we might do, or hope to become in the future, as young lads will, professional shearers was not on the list of things to do. If there's such a place as Hell, they're all shearing sheep down there.

As I said earlier on things haven't changed all that much for the owner or handler of sheep. Take for example the dosing of them. Today a lot of money has been invested in the very latest and best of penning facilities; race / chute, dipping tub, sorting pens, holding pens, shedding gates, the lot. It all looks dead easy, at least for those of us who remember the 'good old day's, but give it a try, and you'll find that the cussed ewe will defy any attempt to make life easy. Picture it if you can a chute full of sheep, a knapsack dosing pack on your back with length of white plastic tubing leading down to the drenching gun in your hand as you commence to dose. The first eight or ten are a piece of cake, and you mentally wonder how you put up for years with chasing them 'round an outhouse with low roof, catching with one hand and a Baby Power whiskey bottle containing dose in the other, sweat dripping off you and the sheep blowing like mad. It's at this stage you run into trouble. You slip your free hand under the next sheep's jaw and proceed to put dosing gun into the side of her mouth. She objects violently, first tries to jump up on the one in front, then does a quick reverse. Finding no slack either way she sits down on her arse thus giving room for the one in front to come back or the one behind to go forward. Either move causes a halt to the smooth running of the job, for one or other has got her legs tangled up in the length of plastic pipe between pack and dosing gun. You're half strangled with the strap of the dosing pack as you try to extricate yourself and keep the gun from being kicked into the next county. As you let go the trigger, instead of more dose coming down the tube as is proper, it sucks up dirt and the whole operation comes to a halt as you head for the tap to wash things out. If this happens more than once, and it does, you're half tempted to look for the Baby Power bottle! At least there's no valves or attachments to get buggered up. The job is quicker, granted, but the sweat you worked up in the outhouse is back on your face.

Some of today's modern doses are given by injection, but that way also has its troubles. The instructions on the bottle make it sound simple, a mere three to five cc to be given. Just pull up some loose skin along the rib cage or neck, slip the needle in and press plunger. I don't know what a ewe does with her loose skin when you go looking for it, but she sure knows how to hide it, and a prod of a needle makes the most docile of them fit to jump Beechers, (a famous horse jump). With all the jumping and movement it's quite easy to give yourself a cc or two of 8 in 1 pre lambing serum. Unless your pregnant it won't do you a bit of good, but you'll have a damn sore hand for a few days.

Another exciting mission is to give 'em a run through the footbath. In my apprenticeship days you chased them around (in the outhouse), grabbed one, turned her up, dumped her on her rump and proceeded to manicure her feet, then paint or pour on an anti- foot rot solution. That operation still has to be done but now you have a catching cage that swings them upside down making the job more manageable; big saving on the back anyway. But the footbath is a different kettle of fish altogether. Ever try a bunch of hoggets (one year olds) that have never seen a footbath. No way will they face into that shining water with maybe a glint of sunshine on it. The ones up front will turn around and face back into the rearguard. Frothing at the mouth you eventually catch one to force her through. Just grab the rails and push hard against her with knee or foot. She'll do one of two things. Back up against you, so's you'll be forced to push her through the full length of the bath, or she'll buck jump through hitting the water about twice and kicking the formula all over you with her hind legs. Eyes stinging with bluestone or formaldehyde you grope around to catch another! It's not an easy task I assure you. Then, when you eventually get 'em running, a smart arsed one will jump up on the backs of the others and fly through never touching the water.

Still in the same up market surroundings having a go at dipping them produces the same exertions and hardships. The holding pen is circular, the idea being, that as the flock moves through the tub you keep moving the gate behind the remainder so as to keep them up nice and tight and handy. A decoy sheep is placed in the pocket, just beyond the slippery slope where they can't possibly stand upright and must fall in of their own violation. So far so good, but if perchance the flock you wish to dip are a bunch of three/four year old ewes you have a problem on your hands. Having been dipped many times these old biddies can smell dip a mile away, and will push and shove and lie up against the gate you are meant to be moving to keep them up tight. Two men with the strength of Samson plus a barking dog will not move them off that gate. Straining heaving and blowing like a porpoise you inch them nearer bit by bit up the tub slope. Eventually in vexation you'll grab one and fling her in. Head first rump first, you don't give a damn, tho' the experts will tell you to ease them in gently, rump first!

Shearing I've already mentioned and it's nice to think that the hand shears is now a collector's item. The new clippers, either electric or engine driven are vast improvements but they haven't yet invented the sit and be quiet ewe. And its time the experts invented a shredder or baler for handling the fleece for it's another back breaking job.

All of the abovementioned chores that can draw sweat from you're brow are centred in the handling area, but the transporting of sheep has its own special 'initiation rites' and they are recurring ever time you drop the loading ramp. You make a start by reversing your new twin-axle stock trailer to the exit loading bay. If there's only a few to be loaded, no problem, they'll fly in, shut up the ramp and off you go. But suppose your loading a full complement, top and bottom deck, now that little exercise can use up some of your time, and a great deal of your effort. As you proceed to load the top deck you run into the first snag. These new modern trailers are roofed over, another sheep benefit; keeps the wind and rain off them. God's truth, they'll be roofing over the fields next! The roof of course makes it quite dark up there and after the first ten or twelve go up it gets darker. No ewe will proceed into the unknown, so the first lot up will turn 'round and meet the next lot coming up as if to get confirmation about that empty dark space up front. It's a real merry - go - round as you push and shout from the back Eventually, you get 'em squeezed in, bar one! As you push hard she decides to get down on her knees and shove in under the others. With front end down and rear end up she pushes with nervous energy and pisses down on you at the same time. Loading the bottom deck is more of the same. It's even darker down there, but you can hoosh 'em along from the air vents at the side. Stick your arm in and push. Up goes the one you're heaving on, as she makes some room up comes the one from behind her, catching your out-stretched arm between her body and one of the iron struts of the trailer. It won't break your arm, but you'll have a bloody big red weal or raze mark down along it. As you move off you glance at the old tractor trailer sitting in a bunch of nettles, the one with the made up sheep sides on it; a couple of lengths of 6x1 board with 3x2's nailed to them on one side, and a length of galvanised sheeting on the other. It sits there in the haggard with a neglected look about it, and as you pass by with a stinking wet shirt and sore arm, you're not in much humour for praising progress.

This story about sheep would not be complete without a mention of the buying and selling of them, for it's a most important aspect. There's an old saying in farm circles; the day you buy is the day you sell, it's an obvious statement and it applies to all livestock. Sheep are bought and sold the round of the year, however the most important sales are the Brood Ewe Sales starting 'round the beginning of August and tailing off come November. It's the time when a farmer's wit replaces his brawn, for he is laying his money down on next years crop of lambs. His choice is wide, both in breed and type of animal he wants, age is also a factor.

Today, unless buying direct, he will go to a modern livestock mart, which advertises brood ewe sales. Strolling along the alleyways before start of sale a farmer casts his eye on what's on offer, and will examine the odd mouth checking on age, and will keep in mind a pen or two worth a bid. It's at this stage the battle of wits between seller and buyer begins, for although the sheep may be sold under the auctioneer's hammer today, as compared to the fair days of years ago, it doesn't prevent the seller from doing a good PR job on his product. Most owners will be hovering near their pen or pens for sale, and if a prospective buyer should stop for a mere moment to look, he has the owner at his side. "If it's a gen-a-wine bunch a yeows ye're looking for, ye needn't go ainy farther", could be an opening gambit. The prospective buyer will not commit himself at this stage, but will give a grunt or nod of approval, pass comment on the weather, and move on. He has other pens to look at. But should he show interest he'll agree they look good , but there's one of them a bit crabby (small). "Nottin da matter with yer eyesight", will come the quick reply. A complement early on is a help to encourage interest!

"Tell ya nottin but da truth now, I was goin to lave her off, but she have triplets last year".

"Tell ya what, if ya buy dem, ya can lave her off, ain't dat fair enough, suit yerself ".

The ball is now in the buyer's court The fact that she had triplets last year is no guarantee that she'll have them this year, but it's a possibility, and if they come right (price wise) she's not all that crabby!

"Ye'll give me a bit a luck if I take her".

"Sure I'd do dat anyroads"

An' so it goes. When the pen comes under the hammer both men have an understanding!

Examination of the mouths and udders is something not to be overlooked. A good udder is free of all lumps and supple. A hogget (yearling) or two year old, is easy enough to recognise, two front teeth up for hogget, four for two year old, but from three on it take expertise. A three year old on good pasture all her life will grow long teeth and become a bit gappy. An old ewe, five or six years and up will definitely have long gappy teeth and this is where difference of opinion and heated argument can arise regarding age. Conversely, a young ewe on hard pickins (mountain grazing) will have worn down teeth, but that can also apply to an aged ewe. A young ewe can have teeth missing from scooping hard turnips. The seller will say it's only her pin teeth (baby teeth) that are missing. The buyer will say "She's as auld as a bush". T'would take the wisdom of Solomon or an arbitration board from Heaven to get either side to agree, but at the at the end of the day supply and demand, as always, will govern what takes place.

So why keep sheep if there're all that trouble? Well, they do have a few things going for them. First of all, there're money earners, if not spectacular, at least steady. They clean up pastures after cattle especially when the land is too wet to carry cattle. They've always been considered great land makers, ideal for grazing new seeded land, (the golden hoof). All things considered, there's nothing much wrong with sheep. They're just too cussed and contrary to fully appreciate all the new fangled ideas and aids we mortals have dreamed up for their convenience!

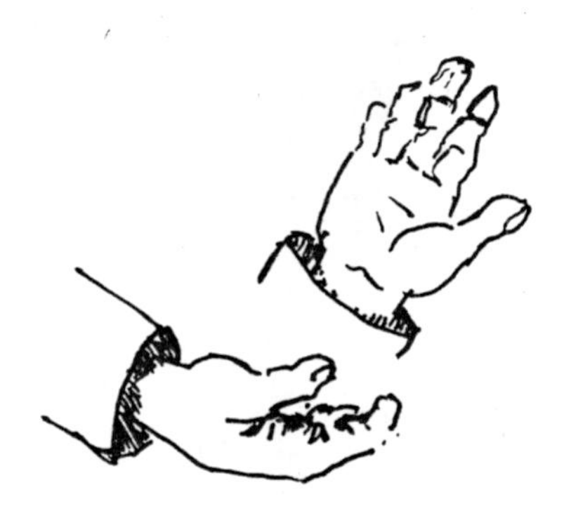

Chapter 18
Fairs Old and New

The business centre for all farmers big or small in those 'good 'ol days' was the Fair Day. Held all over the land, especially in spring and autumn it was the place where livestock of all gender, breed, and description were traded. Not only livestock, but traders selling products ancillary to farming, (horse harness, small hardware) set up stalls at some of the bigger ones, and of course the local hardware shop did good business for a lot of farmers waited till Fair Day to make other purchases. It was a red-letter day for the publicans of the town for manys the deal was finalised in the pub and where money changed hands. In fact it was a good day for the town. Towns folk were up early preparing for the invasion; planks were laid on barrels in front of shop fronts to keep animals away from the windows, but more important to prevent animal waste (shit) from splattering the doorways and windows. Eatin' houses, today called restaurants or cafes, also did a roaring trade. The smell of black puddings and rashers wafting from these places on a cold frosty morning improved the appetite no end, especially if one had walked in animals a distance.

My abiding memory of fairs is one of sore feet and tired limbs. On one occasion myself and the farm boy, (Mick), my shearing partner, were detailed to drove four fat heifers in to Naas fair, a distance of eight miles. Actually they were going direct into Mileys, the butcher. He had come out home a few days previous on a bike, and bought the animals 'by hand'. In those days you had a choice, one could buy by hand or by weight. It was usually by hand as the only weigh scales within shoutin' distance were the public weigh scales in market towns. Not all towns boasted such a luxury.

The fair day was considered a good choice for moving the animals, for with two 'drovers' on the road it was an ideal time to make a purchase or two at the fair and give the Lads something to do on the way home! We set off in high spirits; this was 'mans work' taking place on the public road for all to see. As the animals were mud fat we were under strict orders to 'take them easy', in other words one of us was to stay in front and set the pace. But that way we couldn't 'goster', (idle chat about nothing in particular). A short distance from home we drove from the rear, and the heifers upped the pace a bit being fresh out of stalls and rarin' to go. The inevitable happened . Soon their tongues were out and they were blowing hard. Panting and blowing they got as far as the main street in Naas and there and then decided they'd had enough. They just lay down, well two of did, and the other two just looked on. Curiosity will always draw a crowd even if it's only two fat heifers taking their ease on a main street.

Advice came in abundance and from all directions.

"Wha-deya think ye're at"? A stupid question deserves a stupid answer.

"We're here for the good of our health".

"Well yer health won't improve when the owner comes along". This statement did nothing for our wellbeing. Bad news travels fast and Mr Miley whose premises was further down street was soon on the scene. If he was upset by the situation he didn't show it.

"Lads, lads", he tut tutted, "just let them be, they'll get up in their own time," which of course they did. There and then I think the two of us came to fully understand the meaning of the word tolerance! Mr Miley had it in spades. When they got their second wind they got to their feet, and slowly, carefully, we got them the rest of the way into a small paddock at the back of his premises. Our pride somewhat dented we headed for the fair green at the edge of town and located my Father who was busy finalising a deal for a bunch of store cattle, ones requiring further fattening. Speaking from memory I think the price was £42 pounds a piece (per head): the luck penny was half a dollar 2/6 (two shillings and sixpence) each. Father handed us five bob (shillings) biding us to get something to eat. Five shillings in those times bought a lot of grub, but we ate every penny of it, then started out for home with the new purchases. Arriving home late afternoon footsore and weary, we added 'droving' to 'sheep shearing' on our list of careers not to be pursued.

But there was at that time professional drovers, and they too had their pecking order, or like today, the two-tier system applied. Those at the top operated for big buyers, the rest grabbed work wherever they could get it. Walking the roads by day and late into the night they ambled along at the animals pace. They knew every inch of the road and where they could get a stop for the night if the journey was very long. A shed full of hay was sometimes their bedroom. Barney Noonan, Pat Dwyer. The Whistler Delaney are names that come to mind. The Whistler had a clubfoot and a crooked leg, probably as a result of polio, but he walked the roads with the best of them. Incidentally, I never heard him whistling.

There was one other character in those days that has gone completely from the scene today. He was not involved in the livestock trade as such, nevertheless, he travelled the roads daily in all weathers doing a business that was overlooked by the tanglers and dealers. He had a niche market and it was a profitable one. No matter what territory or locality he worked or lived in he was hardly ever referred to by his real name, but always went by the nickname of 'Chicken choker' or 'Higgler'. We had one in our parish and on any road or at any hour of the day you could meet Billie sitting up in a small spring dray pulled by a small pony, a rug pulled over his knees to keep him warm. If it was morning and he was just starting out, the dray would be empty, but meet him in the evening and the dray would be full of freshly choked chickens and boxes of hens, turkeys, or goose eggs. All farms, big or small, kept poultry and Billie sourced the countryside relieving the farmer's wife of any surplus she might have, for not all wives wished or were physically able to hawk their wares into the nearest town for sale. She probably felt on firmer ground haggling with Billie on her own doorstep as to what the eventually price might be for the product on offer! It goes without saying that the busiest time of the year for Billie was the approach of Xmas. He and his wife plus some outside help would be up to their eyes and literally up to their knees in feathers, plucking turkeys and geese in readiness for the big day. Much of his wares were for butchers in the local towns and some went on to the poultry market in Smithfield, Dublin, or one could buy from him direct at his house.

Without too much formal education Billie followed the financial ups and downs of market forces in the poultry segment and adjusted his prices accordingly. As a consequence of this he drew both praise and derision from his customers; it all depended on the 'highs' and 'lows', or put another way, the supply and demand for the product at time of purchase. If prices were good—"There's no better man to dale (deal) with". "Do ye a turn any day". If prices were bad, —"Jasus, that fella" "Rob ya, he would". It was all the same to Billie, in spite of the ups and downs in the market place he stayed in business. He put the pony out to grass and bought him self a small Ford van and continued to be a 'chicken choker' to the end of his days. His trade and himself have long since passed, taken over by poultry fattening units and super markets. He was one of the 'original middle men' that producer and retailer don't as yet seem to be able to do without, and I think he originally came from Co Cork, so one can only pass him the highest Kerry compliment that's known —He was a 'Cute Cork Hoor'!

To days Livestock Marts appeared among the old Fair Days 'round the mid 1950s and not without a fair amount of opposition. Two sides took up entrenched positions, and meetings were held all over the country running two very different kinds of agenda. Those in favour of, and those widely against. Manys the pub with a smoky lounge did good business

The trading of goods of all kinds, and that includes livestock, has been taking place all over the world since forever. Bartering, haggling, exchanging, whether on the Fair greens of Ireland, the Bazaars of the East, or the corporate boardrooms of the World, the name of the game is the same for all. The seller to get as much as he can, the buyer to give as little as possible. The gap between parties can be large or small depending on a number of factors, and there are a number of ruses used to reduce that gap, but the bottom line is always money.

Like football teams it was a match between the Dealers V The Rest, and the pitches were hotel function rooms or pub lounges. No half time and no referee, but lots of linesmen with plenty of opinions and suggestions, some delivered unobtrusively and some abusively. These matches/meetings took place when there was a hint or rumour of a livestock mart going to be erected. The pub meetings could best be described as training sessions for the two factions i.e. planning strategies, which in plain language meant going to your neighbour next day to bully or cajole him into your way of thinking.

No outsider, or visitor to our shores could possibly understand what all the hassle was about. To those not in the know it seemed better to do your business in the relative comfort of a covered sales ring than stand out in all weathers holding a bunch of cattle up against a shop window or wall. The choice seemed obvious, but far too simple for all the rigmarole and ramifications that went on at those meetings.

Them and Us were roughly divided into two categories, the 'Dalin' Man' (Dealer), and the Farmer. It was a convoluted mish-mash of peoples for some dealers were also farmers. There was a third category, the Cute Hoor, who kept a foot in both camps. Like the weather his opinions were changeable, and if it looked like a vote was coming up at a meeting, and it was always taken on a show of hands, intimidation at its best, he was gone for a pint or a piss!

The Dealer group was the more vociferous, for it seemed

they had the more to lose. Dealing could be described as a three-tier group. Mr Big, who drove 'round the country in the biggest car that could be purchased at the time, and Mr Small, who peddled 'round on a bicycle, usually wanting a set of tires. In between, you had the lads on the way up or down, depending on their abilities. Collectively described as Blockers, Tanglers, or Jobbers, and often referred to with a degree of distain. They all had a part to play in the livestock business, especially the cattle end. The small fry scurried 'round the country, spotting and noting animals fit for sale, about to be sold, where they were, and in what quantity. Coming up to fair day they'd have every animal catalogued so to speak, from the widow woman with one or two, up to the larger holding with ten or more.

These men had honeyed tongues, and in today's modern world would be on the P R lecture circuit. Propping the bike against the wall or hedge of the farmyard he had a couple of opening gambits. The first and obvious one, was to be full of praise of the intended victim, and the second was to work out how he could gain the upper hand of the situation, without the other person realising it.

"Be-gor Missus, ye have the place looking fine",

"Ah tis not too bad, takes a lot a hard work".

"An' no better person than yerself".

She, is on the alert, and knows that the visit isn't just to pass the time a day!

"Tell me, that's a fine lump iv an' animal ye have in the paddock, would ja be thinkin' a sellin'?"

"I might, if I got enough".

"That'll do ye now, don't I allus look after ya."

"Huh, ya robbed me last year".

"I'll do me best for ye, an don't worry about getting' her to the fair on yere own, yer man up the road is sendin' a few an we'll get her in with dem."

The promise of a fair price and transport laid on, is probably enough to tip the scales in his favour.

If he comes up against a tough customer, one who is known locally as well able to fight his own corner, he adopts a subservient manner.

"Dem's a fine a bunch a pollys (no horns) ye have dere in da front field, but sure maybee ye have a road for dem yerself."

This boosts the farmer's ego. Thoughts conjure up in his head of Mr Big himself arriving in his big car into his very own farmyard.

"I had a fella enquirin' t'other day if I had antin." Could be true or false.

"Tell ya what ye'll do, do yer best, but don't let them off without commin' back to me."

The farmer is anxious to keep all roads open, and says he'll get back to him for sure. The Jobber leaves at this stage knowing it's a 50/50 chance, and makes it his business to call back in a short while. If the cattle are still there, the odds have moved 60/40 in his favour. This wheeling and dealing goes on all over the country, but sooner or later most of the animals will arrive at the fair if not under his care, under his eye! Independent farmers will do their own thing, sell at home or at the fair.

On fair mornings all roads leading into town would have their compliment of livestock moving along them, heading for the fair green or main street. This is where the Blocker came into action. Out along the roads chatting up owners and bidding them a bad price. A general softening up process, getting them set up for Mr Big. When the big man himself arrived, his minder gave him the run down on who had what, what was bid, and most important, who the opposition were. Mr Big was always a well dressed fellow, and he and his peers had one thing in common vis-a vis dress; they all wore yalla (yellow) boots. Tan colour I suppose is the correct description but they were always referred to as yalla, and his underlings all aspired to wearing the same badge of office, even if at times they were only hand-me-downs.

There were many permutations of the ringing and rigging that took place at fairs. Not all men who stood with a bunch of cattle were the real owners. The animals would have been gathered up by an aspiring Jobber 'round the countryside and paid for, craftily mixing the dear and the cheap ones. A side-kick was put in charge on the day, told what to ask, and what to take. When an agent buyer for some of the big farms or estates arrived, he was immediately collared by Mr Up-an-Up and directed to the cattle in question. On the way the prospective buyer was fed a long spiel about what good value these animals would be as he himself knew all about them, and how the Johnnie Raw with them was under pressure to sell. In no time at all a deal was done, after a bit of pretend reluctance by Johnnie Raw as to how he wasn't getting out, losing his shirt, robbed, etc. Johnnie got a few bob (shillings) for a few hours work, Mr Up-an-Up got his profit, and the buyer got the cattle, everyone happy. So why such a convoluted way to sell a few cattle? Well, you would have had to ask Mr Up-an-Up that one, and I doubt if you would have got an answer; not a straight one anyway. One possible answer was that Mr Up-an-Up had bought too dear, and had hawked them 'round a couple of fairs to no avail, so the only way out was to plank them with someone, then sell a good story before selling the cattle.

The 'Poor Widda Woman' was another tactic used, and it

worked for either side. A couple of strong weanlings or hairy heifer would be touted to you in whinging manner. "These belong to a widda beyant in the glen, she's in poor enough circumstances the poor crathur, maybe you could see yer way to giving her a good price. A few extra bob (shillings) would be gouged out of you, even if you only half believed the story, for no one took the risk of appearing stingy if perchance it were true, and it was comforting to have the feeling that you were someone who could throw a few bob away and you wouldn't miss it! The other side of the coin was used in the same manner. "I wanta buy a couple a weanlings for a widda woman out da back 'o da hill, and sure you won't be too hard on her." I have often thought that if in those times a census was taken of all the poor farm widda's in the country, they would have make up half the population!

Jobbers, Dealers, Tanglers, call them what you will, but they could read a customer from half way across the fair green and have a spake (word) ready for all situations and circumstances. Modern day philologists would have taught them nothing, for they knew it all. How did they live? Well the short answer is, on their wits, and crumbs from the Captain's table. Spotting, sorting, droving, loading at railway stations, the odd luck penny, and the odd lucky deal for themselves.

If you could combine shady practice with honesty and put a name on it, it would be an apt description of a deal at a fair. You were expected to know what you were about, and if next day found that a bullock you had bought had a hoose cough, or a cow had a blind tit, tough luck. Caveat Emptor was the rule. Nevertheless, a seller, anxious to hold on to a good customer would 'make it up' next time they met, but there was no hard or fast rule to do so.

Arm tugging, hand slapping, the waving of ash plants (walking stick, the mark of a true dealer) dividing the difference, splitting a pound, or ten, or maybe five shillings, all added to the cut and trust of a deal. The Tangler, always at hand to move things to a conclusion worked sometimes for the buyer, sometimes for the seller, but always for himself in the hope of a share out when things were finalised. A luck penny was given to make the deal lucky, usually a dollar or half dollar (five shillings or half a crown in those days) All transactions were settled in cash, no bounced cheques in the good old days! Buyers were advised to the local bank, and when buying was finished cash was withdrawn to settle up the various transactions that had taken place. This 'settling up' usually took place in a pub with the landlord sometimes becoming the final owner of the luck penny!

This was the way of it when the 1950's rolled up. As I said earlier the Dealers had the most to lose in the Livestock v Fairs battle. They didn't have complete control over the movement of cattle and sheep, but they had a fair grasp on it, and it was one they were determined to hold on to. In those days cattle moved a possible twelve times from birth to slaughter and money was earned on each movement. It all added up to a considerable sum, and you could be sure a dealer was involved in most of these movements. A lucrative way of life for some that had been going on forever was not going to be relinquished lightly. It should be mentioned that not all farmers were in favour of livestock marts. There is an old Irish proverb that says: marry on your own dunghill, but do your business far from home! They didn't want their business shouted 'round the ringside. Nevertheless there was always the perception that the farmer came off second best when a dealer was involved. They were considered a cartel

(Irish style). Some sort of change was needed to square things up, and it seemed the livestock mart might be the answer. Slowly but surely auction rings started to appear on the horizon both private and co-operative

Before we leave the Dealer it would be unfair to think that all of them were crooks or shady characters. Many of them were running a good business, with integrity, good will, and ability to pay, in a very competitive and sophisticated trade, and keeping a balance in the ever volatile cattle industry.

In the midst of all this brough-ha-ha some hardy and plucky souls went ahead, erected pens and a ring and were open for business. Some folded, others went from strength to strength and tacked on other business interests along the way. The first marts were primitive affairs. Pens made up of old railway sleepers and two by four rails, a small office sheeted with galvanised sheeting and a galvanised canopy over the rostrum, the customers still out in the rain! Today, you have the modern mart with steel penning, some completely roofed over, drinking troughs, power hose washing facilities, loading and unloading bays, canteen, toilets, and seating round the ringside, all mod cons.

We farmers are an odd lot, and it must be in our genes to bitch and beef on any, and every topic. One that comes to mind when marts started up, was the paying of commission for services rendered. It was a personal affront to many that they should be charged anything. Weren't they doing the mart a favour by bringing in their stock, was the attitude, let the other fellow pay. T'other fellow was equally affronted, wasn't he taking them off your hands and took a crooked one at that, he should be paid for the favour. The wrangling that went on at mart meeting or office counter would have to be heard to be believed. All marts, both Co-Op and Private had their teething troubles on start up, but

I think Co-Ops got the most stick. The private ones made what rules and regulations they thought would work and you could lump it or hump it. The Co-Ops were a different kettle of fish. "Com-it-teee Members" were voted on at public meetings, and a certain amount of politics were working behind the scenes. Put on a fella that might do you a turn, if, and when necessary, and to hell with his abilities to run a mart. Another tricky situation arose when two neighbouring farmers, not on the best of terms with each other were proposed, and only one got elected and the one not elected just bulling to be on. There was one customer gone already. "I wouldn't darken da door a tat place, an dat bollicks runnin it, stickin his nose inta my business".

By the end of the sixties the livestock marts had taken over, and the fairs had become a tourist attraction. Now, due to changed circumstances in the livestock business, it looks as if some marts will also become a tourist attraction. But at time of writing, the Co-Op marts alone are responsible for a gross £680million of the cattle industry. It is a remarkable achievement, and a thought to ponder on is that marts were and are run by men who farm by day and organise the running of their respective marts by night. 'Common sense' is not a bad degree to carry 'round with you!

Chapter 19

The Training of the Collie Pup

There has been a radical change in farming practices. Today it is all specialist farming: cereal growing, dairying, beef producing, vegetable growing, the days of the mixed farmer are practically gone. Anything in between is part time, with the part time job probably earning the bigger income. Farms have increased in size and the numbers involved working the land have diminished. Outside help, the farm worker is history. However, if you are in the livestock end of farming there is one important worker still around, willing and able, the sheep dog. On hill farms he is indispensable, and on the lowlands he can save a lot of footslogging. Anyone who has followed the TV series "One Man and his Dog" will get my drift.

There are many breeds of dog in the world, and all are capable of being trained for something, even it its only house trained. The very minimum is obedience. "Sit", "Come", and any person can teach these two basics. At the other end of the scale we have the highly trained specialist breeds. Gun dogs, guard dogs, sniffer dogs, dogs to take care of the blind, dogs to do tricks at the circus, and last but my no means least the sheep dog. I have to admit to a certain amount of prejudice when mentioning that breed, for they are my favourite dog. Clever beyond human understanding, a good one can read your mind before you open your mouth.

All good dog handlers have one thing in common, endless patience. A little and often, is a good rule of thumb as you go through the various stages of training. Over do any session and he'll get pissed off and sulk; sit there and give you a look as much as to say, been there, done that. In a sense there're no different than human beings, and the intelligent one is only dying to show off, and likes being active. Half the battle in training is trying to quell over exuberance without being oppressive.

Not all dogs are trained by experts and no where does this apply more than to the average farm dog. Practically all farms have a dog of some sorts, the good, the bad, and the ugly. The main function of some of them it seems is to bark when a car arrives, then circle it, sniffing its wheels and cock its leg on one of them, then greet the arrival with tail wagging furiously. Others will bark, stay their distance with hair standing along their backs, a deep growl in their throats. A family pet would probably be a fair description, one who will go out the fields with you and hustle along sheep or cows according to its ability.

Some farmers want a bit more from their dog and will make an effort to further its education. It is at this point where a dog's intelligence shows, and sometimes the lack of intelligence on the farmer's side! Quite often it leaves much to be desired. A good skelp of an ash plant (stick) is often thought to be the quickest way to put manners on a dog. All it does is making the animal wary of its trainer and he will spend most of the time watching out for his own welfare, instead of concentrating on the job at hand. Sometimes, just like us humans, you will get the odd mutt, and the best thing to do with him is to leave him minding the back door. To be fair to farmers, not all have the time or the patience for dog training.

The tale I relate took place on a farm adjacent to ours. T'was early November and a heavy fog was rising off the land encouraged by a weakening sun. We were at the end of a beautiful Indian summer spell, which came compliments of Mother Nature, having dished us out a dismal damp summer. All harvest work had been tidied up; ground had dried enough to get at the spuds and roots. It was also the time of year to take a close look at stock and see what was fit for selling, and what was to be kept for wintering. The fine spell had lifted depression, farmers were in better mood and taking their ease, catching up on things that had been left to one side, such as taking time, like me, to get a close look at cattle or maybe give a young dog a try out! See what he was made of. You could say, "God was in His Heaven, all was right with the World".

I set off up the fields, dog at heel, as the last of the fog lifted and stock became visible. You could hear a penny drop at twenty paces, or a voice at several hundred yards. At a rise in the field I stopped to look, the cattle, having just got up were stretching themselves, and starting to mooch off to have their first bite of the day, but now they stood in a circle 'round me, giving the odd cough and tossing their heads at the dog, who was sitting at my feet all alert, just waiting for one of them to make a false move.

Then I heard it. That voice with the soft Wicklow burr!! "Come heer, come heeer, come heeree, the tone rising a key or two, but still soft. Then suddenly, there came an explosion of words that even the cattle looked up and the dog cocked his ears high. "GO BE DAMNED", were the words uttered, and they could be heard a mile away. Wondering what sort of pantomime was taking place in the field next to me I walked to the mearin' hedge (boundary) and looked over; there on stage were three actors! My neighbour, a tall gaunt man dressed in his usual garb, hat sitting forward on his head, brim pulled well down on his forehead, long gabardine coat, black trousers stuffed into Wellington boots, and a long ash plant (walking stick) in one hand. The second actor was a well bred looking collie pup about nine /ten months old, and the third was a black Angus heifer with a touch of the Kerry breed in her. The give away was the short dangerous looking upturned pointed horns. All three stood around a slough or partially dried up pond covering roughly an acre of ground, but in different positions. The field they were in had been meadowed, and had a good cover of lush after-grass on it. The wet patch had been left for obvious reasons, and now had a blanket cover of dead grasses and weeds. The heifer was bang in the middle, head down, tugging vigorously at the dead cocksfoot grasses and facing the pup, the odd switch of her tail telling all who had any interest that she was on full alert! The pup was on the outer edge of the slough sitting on his haunches, one ear cocked, and one down, tongue going vigorously. He looked like he was working out some sort of strategy to get that heifer to turn so's he could dash in and nip her hind legs, for it was obvious that he had no plans to take on those vicious looking pointed horns. Also on the edge but opposite the pup's side was my neighbour, walloping the ash plant off the ground, swearing and threatening all and sundry, and hoping his tactics would move either the heifer or the pup or both. No dice, so he changed tactic. Dropping his voice ever so low and clicking his fingers he tried to sweet talk the pup up to him. "Come heer, good dog, come on". No go, the pup had his mind make up to keep clear of two things, those pointed horns and that ash plant.

Act 2: change of scene. All this excitement had stirred up the neighbourhood; the neighbourhood of animals that is, for all the cattle in my field having heard the commotion were now strung along the hedge, pushing, shoving, and snorting. All males! A grandstand view of dog training was not their interest, but that slinky black female with the narrow Kerry hips. The lady in question was not without interest. It's not every day a girl has twenty ardent admirers, each one prepared to show undying interest, if not love, in spite of a small operation in their early youth which is supposed to quench sexual desire. In female fashion, she obviously decided on a bit of mild flirtation; with toss of head and switch of tail she left the slough and headed for the hedge, stopping just short to give the ground a paw and let out a love bellow. This was the opportunity the pup had been waiting for. He dived in low clasping his jaws 'round a hind leg. Ardour turned to anger as she let fly with her free leg tossing the pup into the air. He landed running for she had turned and charged, head low, those pointed horns bearing down on him. This added bit of excitement increased the adrenaline flow in the boys my side of the hedge as they bucked and snorted, pucking at one another as if they were establishing a pecking order as to who should first win the lady.

Now it was my turn to become alarmed. No hedge could stand up to twenty beefy Romeos with erotic thoughts on their minds pushing and shoving against it and by now thoroughly hotted up. I tried to move them away but it was a useless exercise for they split up every which way but always getting back to the hedge making efforts to jump or push through. The neighbour quickly saw the predicament and rushed into help. Swinging the ash plant in the manner of a discus thrower he laided it along the ribs of the heifer, quickly dispersing all thoughts of love from her mind as she headed for the gap in the hedge she had originally come through to join up with her own bunch. The pup followed at a discreet distance, keeping well away from that swinging ash plant. In time he grew up to be a useful dog in spite of a haphazard and hazardous training, but on the day, you could say it was a case of keeping a dog and doing the barking yourself!

Chapter 20
The Rescue of Kelpie

Another doggie story that took place on our farm involving almost everyone was the "Rescue of Kelpie". Kelpie was a small brown sheep dog, shy by nature, he was useless working cattle, but excellent with sheep. He and the farm apprentice, (my sheep shearing and cattle droving side kick), set off one morning to check on sheep on an out farm we owned at the time. Out of the corner of his eye while doing a count on the sheep, Mick noticed Kelpie take a dive after a rabbit that had cropped up out of nowhere. Satisfied that all was well with the sheep he started for home, taking a short cut through a very large estate of a thousand acres or more. It belonged to a recluse who kept a large pack of mongrel dogs; dogs that strayed in and stayed. The fact that Kelpie wasn't with him didn't bother Mick, for Kelpie had once been attacked and badly savaged by the said pack. Wild horses wouldn't induce him to cross or enter that land since, but if a human wished to take a short cut, Kelpie trotted around the perimeter of the estate wall meeting up with you at the other side. This time on arriving home there was no Kelpie, and when there was no sign of him for his evening meal, a slight worry settled over everyone. Next morning, no sign, and the morning after, still no sign. By this time everyone in the immediate neighbourhood had been alerted. Doom and gloom had descended on all of us; where could he be, or what could have happened to him? We kids called and searched, but to no avail. Worst of all, he was my Mothers pet, and she fretted the whole time saying half under her breath every so often, "Where can he be"? Even those with no particular connection with him would enquire "Any sign yet"? Mick, who had taken him along on the fateful morning, was devastated, for he naturally felt responsible.

On the third morning Mick was back checking on the sheep. He stood up on some high ground the better to get a count; there was a low bush growing about twenty paces away on his left. While counting he was distracted by a familiar noise. A dog's whine! Looking all 'round he listened acutely, wondering if he was dreaming and had he heard correctly. Then he heard it again, a low whimper, and it seemed to be coming from the middle of the bush. Raising some branches of the bush he observed a large hole, much bigger than your average rabbit hole. Picking up a small stone he dropped it in, it seemed an age before it hit bottom. He whistled, and called out, "Kelp". He got an instant reply, Kelpie's bark Hurrying home, half running half walking he broke the news, and instant rescue plans were set in motion. The pony was hitched to the spring dray, ladder, lantern, spade and slash hook, the rescue tools were thrown aboard, the Boss himself (father) taking charge. The bush was quickly cut, the lantern lit, and the ladder lowered, and there was Kelpie down fifteen feet or so in the bowels of the earth looking not much the worst for wear, but somewhat thinner.

He got a hero's welcome on returning to the farmyard, and the last to welcome him was the woman of the house, my Mother. She had prepared a special meal covered in warm milk, but before he touched it, he buried his head in her apron whimpering and wagging his tail. When she straightened up, tears were streaming down her cheeks.

It transpired that Kelpie had fallen down an old disused icehouse when chasing his rabbit. It had fallen into disrepair, the bush disguising the entrance, and had been forgotten about. After the rescue everyone remembered!

Chapter 21
The Farm Labourer

Oh to be a farm labourer in the rare auld times! Now that all depends on which side of the fence you are gazing from. If you grew up in the relative comfort of those times, with a full belly, clothes to keep you warm, and boots to keep your feet dry, you can afford to look at that past scene through rose tinted glasses. However, if you spent your life struggling to achieve the aforementioned three necessities of life, the whole scene is a horse of a different colour.

Now this rare breed of man hasn't disappeared off the face of the earth, it's just that the whole scene has been altered by agricultural economics. The word labourer has gone from our vocabulary, and the politically correct word is farm worker, and he comes in various guises: Farm Relief Services, Agriculture Contractor, Fencing Contractor, Shed and Farm Building

Erector and he arrives on your farm fully mechanised. The sprong and spade will soon be nailed to the barn door as the mechanical marvels of yesterday, and there won't be too many regrets.

On yer bike, as the saying goes, at the crack of dawn, to peddle several miles and be in the farmyard by 8am. No tea break at ten, lunch break 12 noon till 1, no afternoon break, and quit at 6pm, six days a week and the rest of the time was your own. No holidays except Holy Days, and if you held that exalted position of yardman, well, that used up the seventh day, with a break to say your prayers and maybe take in a local football match, so long as the cows didn't have to wait too long for the evening milking. Another form of transport to get you to the job was shanks mare (walking) across the fields. This mode had you limbered up if you were going to follow a pair of horses all day behind a plough or harrow! Another big advantage to walking to work was that if you sat on a tractor all day without cab on it, let alone heater, your feet were warm twice in the day; coming to and going home from work And speaking of walking, a form of medieval torture were the working man's boots. The uppers were made of hard unyielding leather, thick soles also unyielding, with two rows of nails all 'round the outside of the sole, and three rows down the middle, with an iron heel tip on the heel. Made to last forever it seemed, and it took many wettings, with the odd drop of neadsfoot oil before they yielded to the shape of the foot. Meantime plenty of blisters on toes, heels, and ankles

The hours were long the work hard for it was 95% manual, in fact it was probably 100%, because for the life of me, I can't think of any job that didn't entail physical exertion. The remuneration for these efforts was pitiful. Eighteen shillings per week for male adult, and five shillings per week for a young lad having left school at fourteen, if he had stayed that long. I won't convert these sums into present day money for nobody would believe me! This wage increased slowly, and in the mid forty's a statutory wage of twenty four shillings per week was made mandatory. Every farmer thought he'd go broke in the effort to pay it!

As I mentioned earlier there were some perks to be had such as free milk and firewood, and a drill or two of spuds depending on length of drill. There were other bits and bobs for the permanent man. Surplus apples, a bag or two of turnips, the odd chicken or turkey at Christmas and hand me down clothes and foot wear, not forgetting the odd egg lifted from under the hen on the way home. Very often it was the farmer's wife who kept a weather eye on the welfare side of things at least that was so in my Mothers case. There were variations on these arrangements, and they differed from farm to farm.

All these perks were welcome, but the logistics of moving firewood from wood to fireside took planning and effort. If the worker was lucky enough to own an ass and cart and to have a son aged nine or ten it worked this way. Son arrived with transport just before quitting time, then, both of them got stuck into the tree or branch, cut and loaded an ass load then started for home. The distance could be just down the road, or three or four miles. Not a bad way to pass the time of a summer's evening, but just think of a cold winter's night, having already worked all day in similar conditions! Another form of transport was the bicycle. A length of log stretching from saddle to reaching out over the handlebars was often manhandled homewards in this fashion. Next time we reach for the phone to order a 1000 litres for the central heating, spare a thought for yesterday's man.

Before the statutory wage came in, aye, and even after it,

there was always a certain amount of wheeling and dealing to arrive at a figure suitable to both parties. Mick, the young lad who came to work for us at the advanced age of thirteen maybe fourteen was a case in point. The first year or two he was a sort of go-for. Fetch this, get the other, dig the Missus a bucket of spuds for the dinner, or go for a bucket of spring water, especially on butter making days, all the time getting bigger and stronger. He and my Father had one thing in common; a quick temper. He was fired on the spot many times, but after a cooling off period reconciliation was always arrived at and Mick returned, usually with a sweetener in the pay packet to cement the new deal. Between the comings and goings the calendar of time moved on and Mick arrived at eighteen years of age, entitled to the full adult wage of eighteen shillings per week, when in his estimation he pulled off his best stroke. He settled for fifteen shillings per week plus his dinner. He felt he could easily eat his way through the difference in a week!

Turning dung, pitching hay, carrying baskets of turnips into tied up stall fed cattle was all part of the job; the farm worker took it in his stride. The busy periods were spring seeding, haying and harvesting, and they were busy times, when work went on from dawn till dusk, especially during a spell of broken weather when every dry hour was availed of. Official overtime was unheard of; a bonus of a pound or so was given, usually at the end of the busy time, probably a bit extra at Christmas. Cutting thistles, trimming hedges, fencing, and catching up on jobs that had been put on the long finger, filled the slack periods.

There was a pecking order of sorts, especially on larger farms where men were designated specific jobs. The ploughman usually attended to all horse related jobs, the yardman to livestock, and the general handy man who got stuck into anything and everything. When tractors arrived on the land this was definitely a specialist job, and with the Irish penchant for tinkering this job was passed to the fella who could wield a lump hammer and could recognise a left hand thread from a right hand one.

Because a lot of the work involved muscle power, ways and means were devised to lessen the load! Mick and myself were dispatched one morning to sow grass seeds in a field of twenty acres. Father got us started, showing us how to calibrate the seed drill and then went to the races. A man powered grass seed barrow is a simple enough machine comprising a long narrow box of ten or twelve feet sitting on a cradle. A shaft from the land wheel drives a gearbox, which in turn drives a long shaft running the length of the seed box. that has brushes spaced on it every six inches sweeping out the seed through slots that are adjustable. No convoluted instruction book to explain the workings of this Hi-Fi science machine were needed! From past experience the opening in the seed slots were determined by the width of two matches from a McGuire and Patterson Friendly matchbox. These were considered the proper settings necessary to sow 30lbs to the acre, give or take a bit of adjustment. Pushed by hand it was light and easy going on firm land; pushed through four or five inches of loose soil took a bit more effort! The field we were in was of the later kind with two thirds of it level then sloping off steeply.

We had two choices when starting out. Either push the barrow turn about, or, add a length of rope to the front with one of us pushing and in control of the steering, the other pulling on the rope like a jackass. We elected to use the push-pull method and started off at the level end using a straight running fence to get a good line. With about an acre down and the sun shining hotly and the sweat rising, we paused on the headland to take a breather, and to suss out an alternative method of propulsion. The Boss was gone to the races and a pony stood idle below in the stable yard! In no time at all the pony was hitched to the barrow, and with one on the handles in charge of steering, and one leading the animal, the work proceeded at a hot pace for the pony was a fast stepper. Coming near quitting time all three of us had arrived where the field started to slope steeply, and extra effort was required. The pony leaned into her collar a bit more, and the lad on the handles concentrated harder on the steering. But it was time to stop, what hurry was on us, the weather was set fair, sure an hour in the morning would finish it.

Next morning Father went out to the field to view progress. Not noticing the hoof tracks he was astounded, to say the least, at the amount of ground covered, and arriving back in the yard showed his pleasure by splitting the team. He ordered me to yoke the pony to the pony trap and took me with him to look at cattle on the out farm, sending Mick to finish the sowing of the grass seeds! That's what's called, the luck of the draw!

Another job long gone and good riddance, was the packing of old meadow hay into the stable loft. The stable loft was advanced thinking at that time. Along one side holes were cut directly over the hay manger underneath. It was a simple matter to push the hay down through the holes into the manger, thus eliminating pitching and carrying all winter long. But getting the hay into the loft was not a simple matter. Old meadow hay was full of little insects called fenians. You couldn't see them, but you could sure feel them. As usual, it was the younger members of the team that were put up into the loft to pack the hay to the top of the rafters. Eaten alive with fenians, smothered with dust, eyes and nose streaming, one came out of there coughing, spluttering, and gasping for air. Farmers Lung must have originated in such places, but the workers were unaware of it and dust masks were unheard of.

There were two categories of farm worker, the constant and the casual. The constant, as you may guess was a permanent one, the casual moving from job to job following the seasons work. Regardless of the size of farm there was always the specialist; rick and pike (cock) builder, semi-tradesman, (one who did repairs around the place) a jack of all trades, very often the owner himself if the farm was small, and he would be on call on other farms for his special abilities. With or without special abilities all men took a keen interest on what was going on, not only where they worked, but keeping tabs on the surrounding farms and their progress. In spite of hard work and low pay they all took pride in the job and were not without engaging in a bit of one-up-man-ship. One could turn in for work some morning and inform the Boss that he had heard "ere last night", that a neighbour "was planning on knockin' a meadow come the week end." It was a way of telling the farmer to get a move on and get his cut before the neighbour. You don't have to go on a PR course to learn diplomacy! In short, they liked working for a 'headline setter'. To be first at the hay or harvest was important, but to finish before the weather broke was even more important.

On a lighter note it wasn't all hard graft and sweat for the labouring man. Young fellows kicked football or hurled in the long summer evenings, laying down coats for goalposts. Some of them were good enough to be picked to play for the local team some to go on and play for county teams. Handball was also an option if you were lucky to live near a handball alley, but the event that caused greatest excitement and rivalry was the local field day. They have almost disappeared having been upstaged by the County Show, with horse, pony, and livestock events being the main attraction. The ones I refer to gave local talent a chance to show their paces. Foot races, sheaf pitching, tug-a war teams, greasy pig catching, all events giving a man a chance to show muscle combined with skill. Unbe'noanced to anyone and known to everyone, it was surprising the bit of sly training that went on before the big day. Fellas were seen taking a dash across a hayfield, or firing sheaves up in the air for no apparent reason. There were only two conclusions to be drawn from that sort of caper. He was getting ready for the Big House (asylum) or the Big Day! Some trained quite openly, and with more gall than ability threw down challenges to all and sundry. One such challenge was accepted in a harvest field where men were stooking oats. It was lunchtime and they were heading to the yard for their break. The Braggart was telling all who were within hearing distance about his abilities and prospects for Sunday week, all been spared. "Ye wouldn't run a message", came the taunt from a migrant worker who was in the parish doin' casual work. "Who sez so?" came the bellicose reply. "I'se do," says the migrant, "an I'se hav a shilling here that sez I'se bate ye to the gate." "Yer on." A line was drawn in the stubble clay and challenger and challenged stepped up to it. At the drop of a hat by the self appointed starter they were off. Little specks of dust rose from the heels of the contestants as they sped down the field towards the gate, the migrant on the shoulder of the braggart. With thirty paces to go the migrant drew level and nudged the shoulder of his opponent knocking him off balance. Losing pace he tripped over himself and pitched head first into a stook, sheaves falling in all directions he among them. Howls of laughter and derisory comment rose from the spectators.

"Jasus Pat I thought you'd hav left im standin'.

"Ya shudda waited till ye got da dinner". Advice was given

and suggestions offered all through the lunch break. Everyone had their two bits worth of say.

"If ye had a bit a practice, I'd say ya'ed bate da best of im."

"Mebbe ye should take a week off an' rest up".

"Dats right, I seen in da papers where dem top runnin' lads suffer from da nerves, an' hafta rest affores a big race."

The jibes petered out, and for the rest of the afternoon it seemed like the braggart had taken a vow of silence!

Everyone was up and at it come Field Day, which was usually on a Sunday. Chores were done up quickly, early Mass got, and people headed for the sports field. Probably one of the main attractions was the tug-of-war, for neighbouring teams would be taking part, and it was important for the home team to do well. Men and boys stripped to the waist to take part in the various races and events, urged on by their supporters. The man with the loud - hailer was a busy one; calling for entrants for the various events, and then getting them started. People only half listened to what he was saying, for they were too busy watching something else, or just plain gossiping. Some arrived to take part when the event was over, and that caused heated argument.

"Jasus I'da won dat"

"Well ye'll hafta wait till next year now, won't ye."

"I nevir heard ya call out for it."

"Get yer ears washed out, I was tired shoutin' it."

Disgruntled, the late entrant would walk away telling all and sundry that he was a dead cert for it. When the tug-a-war teams were called everyone paid attention and gathered 'round the war zone. Fans and admirers of the participants offered words of encouragement and loads of advice.

"Pull da boots offa dem".

"Pull da shit outa dem."

If the home team got to the finals or even the semi-finals that was acceptable, but woe betide them if they went out the first round.

"Cripes, yis wouldn't pull da skin offa boiled milk."

"Ther's more muscle an' mate 'tween da eyes iv a herrin' den da lot a yis."

"Next year I'll git da granny to giv yis a pull."

The sheaf pitching contest was another event that brought out lots of derisory comment.

"Get it up an over Tom, for God's sake."

"If he were in the bed he would."

"He musta bin dere last night."

These comments would be directed at the father of a large family and brought titters of laughter and more sly insults If perchance women folk were within hearing, sly glances would by cast in their direction to see it they had picked up on the innuendos.

The Big Day over, things would be back to normal next day, but it provided food for gossip for sometime after. Who won what, who nearly won, and who got a roll at the back of the ditch when the sun set! Talk is cheap they say, and it was the one commodity the labouring man could afford in plenty.

There were other forms of entertainment that didn't cost a penny. Chasing after rabbits of an evening with a couple of terrier dogs. A bit of ferreting, pitching horseshoes, gathering at a crossroads of a summers evening to swap yarns and gossip. The only things seen at a crossroads these days are Stop and Yield signs! If a few pence were available a game of 'pitch an toss' might start up. The coming of winter and the short evenings closed off these pastimes. There was little enough doing to pass the time in winter, but mitchin' (visiting) from house to house took place. There was always the popular house on those rounds where a game of cards might start up. Three fifteens, or twenty five were the popular games. To the uninitiated, the explanation of the rules of these games would fill a large column. The best way to learn, but not necessary the cheapest way, if money is on the table is to get instruction from a skilled player. We Irish are a musical people and in many's a cottage rested a fiddle or melodeon (accordion) to be taken down the odd night and a bit of entertainment laid on, be it winter or summer.

These were the times that were in it for the labouring man up to the late forties early fifties, and already there're hard to credit. Today, big efforts are being made to retain our heritage and culture. Interpretative Centres, Folk Museums, Heritage Centres; the reclaiming of old gardens and farmyards and rightly so, for already those times are only a memory for those of us still around to remember.

Chapter 22

The Farm Labourers Wife

When talking about the farm labourer one must include their womenfolk; wives, daughters, sweethearts, for they too pulled their weight in the effort to make ends meet. A few extra bob (shillings) earned, helped to buy schoolbooks for the kids, or shoes, but most important of all was to help put grub on the table. Times were harsh for the workingman and his woman in rural Ireland as recent as forty or fifty years ago. No signing on for welfare if you were out of work and if you were in work wages were a pittance.

Whatever about the rights or wrongs of emigration it has been the safety valve for the workingman down through the years and it enabled those who stayed behind to keep above the bread line, — just about. A country stocked with plenty of food and the good things of life is not worth a damn to anyone with no money in their pocket, and money was the one commodity the farm working man or woman were mighty short of. Twenty four shillings per week was the statutory farm wage in the mid forties, and out of that some paid a rent as high as ten shillings per week for a cottage. That left fourteen shillings (70p) for food, or anything else you might fancy!

Today, we are very conscious of the rights of man and equality for women, and demanding those rights. Maybe they were always there, buried deep in our Constitution, (i.e. all children of the Nation treated equally) but I doubt very much if ever a working man or woman was seen pouring over the Articles of our Constitution by candlelight on a cold winter's night to see if and where they could improve their lot. The gap between what is written on a piece of paper, and reality, is very wide indeed! Some would say things haven't changed much, but generally speaking we are a much better off nation today. When did you last see children going to school barefooted?

So what sorts of job opportunities were open to women from the labouring classes? Some farmer's daughters would also have the same problem. Again, J B Keane poignantly expressed the situation facing a majority of them in another play; 'Sive' The field was limited. Well you could become a teacher, nurse, or join a nunnery. The first two vocations cost money to enter, so those two roads were closed off for the majority, leaving only the pathway to heaven. Not being of that persuasion or gender I cannot comment further, but I sometimes think that the thought of getting a decent meal and proper clothes to cover you and keep you warm, must have been deciding factors when making the decision to become a bride of Christ.

Next opportunity down the line, and provided your credentials were impeccable, was a job in the Big House. Once in you could start off at the bottom, scullery/scrub maid, and if ambitious work your way up through the ranks. Kitchen maid, parlour maid, housemaid, housekeeper, or you could hold sway in the kitchen by becoming a cook. The big snag in trying to land a job in the Big House was that the Big House itself was fast disappearing off the face of the land, and those that were left were carrying our cost cutting exercises such as double jobbing staff, so you could find yourself qualified for everything and nothing. Another choice, if you could call it choice, was to land a job with a farmer's wife helping out on busy days, such as wash days, spring cleaning, or butter making day. These jobs were more or less casual; one or two days a week. Some of them could be on a more permanent basis, it all depended on the wealth of the farmer. One other golden opportunity was to work in the fields. Thinning roots, picking fruit, cutting sheaves at thrashing time, helping out at lambing, or where a herd of cows were kept becoming dairymaid. T'was often said that a cow gave down her milk best when touched by the hands of another female. Fellow feeling I suppose.

Being a dairymaid carried responsibility and a degree of skill was required. She was in charge of the pantry, skimming cream off large pans of milk, putting it into cream crocks where it sat until ripe and ready for churning. The making of butter required not only skill, but also a great deal of effort. Beating, pushing, turning, patting, and squeezing out surplus watery milk with two large butter boards one in each hand; then shaping it into pound blocks, popping it onto a scales, adding or scraping off a bit to reach the required weight. She might also have the added duties of feeding the skim milk to calves or pigs keeping an eye on their welfare, and watching out for scours or anything that might affect their thriving.

At all or at any times a girl could enter into that holy estate of matrimony, there to enter the poverty trap with her fellow feminists of scrimping and scraping. A continuous treadmill of trying to keep grub on the table for her man, herself, and a brood of children. Marry and multiply was church teaching, and God help them in their ignorance, the only rhythm they seemed to understand was the rhythm of a cellie band.

The one thing to be avoided at all costs was to avoid getting 'knocked up'. Methods of contraception were not so sophisticated as present times, and whipping it out at the last second, or taking a quick pee at the back of the ditch after the act took place were haphazard in the extreme. With rare exception, to bare a child out of wedlock seemed at the time to be the ultimate sin. Our Island of Saints and Scholars with Mother Church in control countenanced unprecedented steps of cruelty to have the unfortunate creature banished from home and parish, in the pretence that these things didn't happen, while our knee bending, ring kissing, forelock touching politicians looked the other way. Out of sight out of mind was a ready answer. To be denounced and in some case's disowned by kith and kin must be the ultimate sin. To be fair, some families closed ranks and gave the girl the protection she needed. Another child in an already large family didn't make much difference one way or another. The story put about, would be that the girl's mother had had 'an afterthought'. In spite of winks and nudges the story was accepted. It's an ironic thought, but the day may not be far away when we'll have more single than married mothers!

Another hardship endured by our rural mothers and grandmothers was the lack of running water in the homes. This was commonplace, not only in the labourer's home but also in sizeable farmhouses. Nevertheless the cottage dweller was the hardest hit. A three roomed cottage with thirteen kids, plus Ma and Pa was not unheard of. Just think, in to days terms, of the amount of water needed for drinking, cooking, and general ablutions in such a household. The only accessible water was well, stream, or council pump. If you were lucky, water might be only a few yards away, but it could equally be five hundred yards. It's understandable if not acceptable why the term, 'The Dirty Irish' was coined.

Adversity breeds ingenuity they say, and never more so then when it came to cobbling up ways and means to secure a household water supply. Guttering on the house was an obvious source, and a tar barrel (45galls) was always stuck under the down pipe, but its success depended on inclement weather, a thing not unheard of in Ireland! Where did the tar barrel come from one might ask? In past times the ingredients for road repairs were mixed on site, tar and crushed stone. When empty, the barrels were left by the roadside for later collection. An enterprising cottager would latch onto one, pour in a drop of paraffin oil and put a match to it burning it clean, as good as new. With a touch of paint and stuck under the down pipe you had a supply of water, provided it rained fairly frequently. Water for cooking and drinking came from a well or council pump. In those simple times the housewife was blessed with a choice of water. Well water (hard), and rain water (soft). One for drinking and one for clothes washing. In dry weather if a heavy shower fell every available pot, pan, bucket and basin, was stuck outside to catch that scarce commodity. Water wagons were hammered together by the man of the house and came in two models, standard and deluxe. Four old pram wheels at each corner of a flat platform and pulled by a length of rope was the standard model. Bicycle wheels with drawbar was deluxe.

Either model had a barrel on the platform, and some boasted a cast off milk churn complete with lid. The ubiquitous barrel had one other important function. Two thirds full with a kettle of boiling water to take the chill off, it made an ideal outdoor bath for the man of the house. If per chance a laurel bush hid it from view of prying eyes so much the better!

Daily in our papers or on radio/TV we read of some form of agitation going on about something or other. Changes wanted in the education system, more and better housing, law reform, it goes on and on. The one that must bring a wry smile to the faces of those who worked the water barrel system is the demand for the abolition of water rates. People seem to be personally affronted for being asked to pay for the privilege of turning on the tap in their kitchen / bathroom; a luxury unheard of less than fifty years ago in some cottages.

Water and the careful use of it, was a constant problem for the cottager's wife, but no more so, then the problem of money and how to get it, and this is where the bit of casual labour fitted in. From Spring through to Autumn women were out in the fields, thinning and weeding roots, turning hay round the headlands of meadows, pitching sheaves and cutting them at thrashing time, or taking over the milking while the men stayed late out in the fields during a fine spell. If the work was casual so was the hiring.

"Hi Missus, the turnips are ready for thinning, would'ya have an' interest?"

"I surely would Sir, how much ya payin'?"

"Two bob a drill."

"I'll be down after seein' to the childer."

This deal was struck on the side of the road between my Father and the wife of a man who worked for us. She was on her way home from the dentist having had half her top teeth pulled that morning. By afternoon she was on her way down the first drill, each drill about three hundred yards long. She managed two drills per day along with her household chores and tending to her children. Four shillings per day six days a week totalled twenty four shillings, a welcome addition to her husband's weekly wage. They were a two income family as long as the thinning lasted! This extra cash was carefully nurtured, schoolbooks, a pair of shoes, and maybe a bit put away for Xmas.

Visual advertisement is the best kind, and this woman was never short of work; neighbouring farmers also had roots to be thinned or weeded. Sometimes these jobs took extra effort, for they entailed pushing a pram across pasture fields to get to the root field. With one in the pram, one in the oven, and one trotting along beside her, you could say she wasn't short for company! This woman started her working career as a general factotum (dog's body) in a city household for five shillings per month, plus board. Arise at 5am and finish 'round midnight. Any broken crockery was deductible from the pay packet. Life down on the farm, if not actually Heaven, was definitely not Hell!

As already mentioned, putting grub on the table for a man doing manual labour out in fresh air all day, plus a bevy of kids, was no mean feat. No small families in those days. Rarely was meat on the table unless the husband was good at snaring rabbits. The bulk of the diet was spuds, tho' the famine was over ninety years ago. Spuds, turnips, and cabbage, plus bread and tea were the staples.

During wartime tea was scarce, so tea leaves were well drawn, and fresh leaves were added to existing ones in the pot. Spuds left over from one meal were re-heated in dripping (lard) for the next Practically all folk, from big farm to lowly cottage lived off the land; from large field to cabbage patch was cultivated. Where space allowed a few hens could be seen scratching 'round the cottage doorway, or in the adjoining fields. Mother was attuned to the plight of her fellow feminists, and sent the odd chicken or a few eggs or a jar or two of black current jam to the wives of men who worked on our farm. This jam was not to be used in extravagant fashion, such as spreading on dry bread, but a spoonful each night in a mug of hot water and given to each child helped keep away colds and flu when winter approached. It was a way of giving vitamins before multi-vitamin capsules were available.

Probably one of the busiest women in a rural parish at the time was the mid-wife. Peddling 'round the district up hill and down dale in all weathers her black bag strapped on behind, she was as well known as 'the beggin' ass'. Families were large compared to present times and barring complications a lot of babies were born at home. Babies, like calves or lambs do not give a very accurate forecast of their arrival, hence it was an around the clock profession. If caught out late at night with a difficult or prolonged birth, it was not unknown for her to slip in beside mother and new-born for a few hours rest, then rise and get breakfast for the other members of the family, while mother and child rested, before she went on her way. Say what you will, but those times were tough and arduous for the rural workingwomen be they married or single.

For the married one, keeping food on the table and clothes on the backs of her family were her main occupations. 'Hand me downs' were the order of the day; shoes and boots were kept for wintertime. Bare feet, were the summer fashion wear in a lot of cases. To be a good needlewoman was a big help, and if her man was handy with a boot last so much the better. Old bicycle tires cut to shape replaced leather soles on footwear when the original soles wore out.

Entertainment was scarce; gossiping with neighbours and friends after Mass on Sundays, or out shopping. The occasional trip to the pictures or local drama group; four pence got you into the gods (cheap seats) and in summer time there was always the local field or sports day.

Her single counterpart wasn't much better off. Those who made it to the teaching, religious, or nursing professions were considered to be on the 'pigs back'. The rest headed for the Big House, farmhouse, or a 'behind the counter job' in the local town and some to the city. There was always the boat to England or further afield, but England was the preferred choice. It didn't cost that much to get there, and there was always a cousin, brother, sister, or some connection to help get you a start.

To-days rural women have different values, different pressures, and have come a long way from those times. May they remember their sisters of yesterday, for some could be their mothers, and certainly not later than their grandmothers; women whose forbearance and resolute manner have contributed in no small way to the status of present day rural woman.

Chapter 23
The County Show

There are many manifestations of the County Show, as distinct from the Field Day, which I have already mentioned. Small ones are usually run by local farm groups such as Macra or 4H clubs, the bigger ones taking in the whole County, and then there are the huge ones such as The Royal Show in Scotland, Stoneleigh in England, and our own RDS, which itself has been somewhat superseded by the Ploughing Match, as much a trade and stock show as a ploughing competition. Regardless of their size or sophistication they all take an enormous amount of planning and behind the scenes activity to make them a success on the day. Sponsors have to be found, for these shows large of small cost money to run. Then entrants for the various classes have to be sought out. Horses, cattle, sheep, pigs, goats, poultry and farm produce, it's a tall order. Committee people and their helpers scour the countryside looking and asking for suitable entrees. This is not such a problem for the larger ones because a lot of their entrants come from the smaller ones, where a rosette of some colour, or a mention, has fired ambition. Stewarts to be nominated,judges to be picked with great care, and preferable living far from the action centre. Partisan views can cause local feuds!

Modern communications must make the workload of today's committee person a lot easier. A phone in every farmhouse and a mailman to deliver the entry forms; these to be returned with entry fee, postal order or cheques accepted, no cash please. Years ago things were more laid back. Church and chapel gates of a Sunday were good communication centres.

"Ye'll have something for us for the big day."

"Ah, I suppose so, how's it commin along anyways?

"Good, I have a few calls to make yet."

One of these 'few calls' concerned my Father. He was breaking a young horse in the back haggard one day when this fellow drove up.

"God bless the work," was the opening gambit.

"God bless the man," replied Father, wondering to him self what this fellow was selling.

"Them is as fine a bunch a Angus heifers as I ever laid eyes on out there in the field, I stopped to admire them on me way in, prize winners all."

Father reigned in the horse and came alert, if this fellow was a buyer the price was going up with every utterance. His next sentence cleared the confusion. "Ye'll enter a couple a them for the Show." Father was now caught between a rock and a hard place; the caller had done his homework well! Having had the animals praised to the heights, he could hardly say he hadn't anything good enough and it would be churlish to give a flat refusal. "I'll give it a think," was as far as he'd go and the scout left, convinced that he had another entry!

A man of instant impulse, a week before the Show Father ordered Mike and I to bring in the heifers from the front lawn. There were a dozen of them, mud fat. On today's fat scale all 05's. He picked out two, one jet black, one blue grey, and we put them in a house, and the others were turned back out to the field. They say a week is a long time in politics, but it's not nearly long enough when it comes to taming two wild Aberdeen Angus heifers that never had a hand laid on them since date of birth. The training sessions were not allowed upset the normal farm work and took place every evening after supper.

Not all rodeos take place in the Wild West. We had one in our yard every evening of that week, thrills and spills a plenty! Somehow or other we got halters on them, which were cut down horse head collars, and tried every evening to get the Ladies to walk along beside us in best show ring fashion. Someone suggested with tongue in cheek that we should get a photo of docile pedigree animals ring walking, and show it to our pair. We were not amused. But truth to tell, as hardy young farm lads of the time, we enjoyed it. We also had one big advantage; we were lean and fit, and the Ladies were carrying top weight, about 560 kgs of it or 11 cwt in old language. After the initial start up tussle they'd start to blow and were more amiable to instruction. We named them Blue and Blackie.

There were no jeeps or stock trailers in those days so the local trucker was booked, and he arrived at the appointed time with lots of clean straw on the truck floor. More was added, and the Girls loaded up beautifully. Arriving at the Show grounds we were shown our holding pen, which was made up of farm gates and stakes at each corner. A short distance away men and chaps were erecting a parade ring which consisted of 6ft stakes driven into the ground to form a circle. A long length of rope tied to them made the circle. A farm trailer was parked along side for the dignitaries to stand on

We gave the Girls a final rub down and they laid into the hay we dropped at their heads. Two more docile beauties you never laid eyes on. We were pretty smart looking ourselves, Mick and I. No jeans in those days we were dressed in our Sunday best. In typical Protestant dress mode I wore grey slacks, blue blazer with white shirt, collar turned out. Mick was dressed in his new LDF (Local Defence Force) trousers and shirt, and wearing highly polished black army boots. This was forward planning on our part for there was a Show dance that night; naturally we wished to impress the local talent!

The judges moved along the holding pens accompanied by a steward with clipboard in hand taking notes. Everyone waited with baited breath for the call to the parade ring where the final decisions were taken. Get to the parade ring and you were in with a good chance. Presently, another steward climbed aboard the farm trailer and with loudhailer proceeded to call out the numbers to go to the ring. Blue and Blackie's numbers were called and we started to make out way there albeit in a circuitous fashion, for the crowds and commotion had an unsettling effect on our Ladies. With some coaxing, and a lot of pushing and prodding from neighbours willing us on to victory we got there. We hadn't won anything yet, but word was out,—t'was a foregone conclusion. "Sure dem judges i'd be blind, if they missed dem two." We did a circuit of the ring then got called out to the centre. Excitement ran high. Then disaster struck! One of the judges gave it as his opinion that Blue was in calf. To be eligible for the class she was entered in she had to be maiden. All verbal hell broke loose. My father was furious. Not only was Blue's virginity in question, his integrity was in doubt. Not known locally as a man to pull a fast one, his honour was now being put to the test in the public glare. He challenged the judges, the Show committee, and anyone else who wished to lose money to put their money where their mouths were. He'd bet his bottom dollar on Blue's chastity. There were no takers; instead an independent assessment was called for. There's one in every parish; an expert! This man, in dairying all his life stepped forward. Well used to handling livestock he slapped his hand between Blue's legs to check her tits for wax, a sure sign of a heifer in calf. The indignity of it! No lady likes having her tits handled in public and Blue was no exception. She let fly with a hind leg and the expert crumpled to the ground clutching at the private parts of his anatomy. The bovine answer to sexual harassment.

To this day I don't know what triggered Blue's next move. It was probably a combination of the crowd pressing in around her, the noise, and been handled with impropriety. With a toss of her head, a switch of her tail, she spotted a gap in the ringside crowd and bolted for it, knocking me off my feet. The crowd split with the speed of light. Kids were thrown to safety; ladies in high heels buckled over, in their mad dash to get out of the way, men hupped and hawed. I hung on grimly as we both headed for the boundary hedge, wrapped in a tangle of rope and stakes that was once a parade ring. If there was a prize going for grass skiing I was definitely in for a red rosette. She came up short at the hedge and away from the madding crowd immediately started pulling on the fresh grass that grew there as if she'd never seen a bit in her life. I picked myself up. A mixture of cow shit and fresh green grass did not enhance my appearance. Buttons gone from the blazer, the flannels a greeny grey colour not to mention the smell, made my chances at the Show dance zero. Father ordered the trucker to the loading bay and all headed home. An ignominious end to what had otherwise promised to be a gala day and night.

A couple of days later Blue was sold to the local butcher. Father went to the slaughterhouse to prove a point. There was no calf. Honour was satisfied.

Chapter 24
The Gunner Ryan

In this modern age we now live in they never seem to get a mention, perhaps they have all disappeared, but in the old days every parish had its share of them. I speak of 'characters' and our parish wasn't short of them. The 'Joult' Doyle, the 'Badger' Doyle, 'Thrush' Neal, (pronounced Nail) 'Sledger' Nail, and the 'Gunner' Ryan. Each and every one of them had nicknames, usually acquired by the occupation they had followed through life or for some other obscure reason possibly forgotten. The Gunner was such a one. A tall well built man of middle years he had spent some time in the army, hence his nickname. Neat clipped moustache and crew cut hair he induced a military presence in any company he stood with, coupled with the fact that he always wore a brown army fatigue jacket, minus some of the brass buttons. He got by doing 'bits and bobs' 'round the town, that, and a small army pension plus a dole pittance kept him in porter money first and grub second. He wasn't really lazy; he just had no plans to become a millionaire. He had once worked for a farmer and made a pledge with himself never again. People had heard of slave labour camps, he boasted that he had worked in one! His spell in the army had taught him a few tricks; he'd learned how to dodge the column. But life has a funny way of playing tricks on one's options when it comes to earning a few bob. In spite of his pledge to himself, the Gunner on this occasion found himself standing in the middle of a field of oaten stooks on a sweltering hot day praying for rain!

Way back in God's time long before the advent of the combine harvester the saving of a field of grain was quite labour intensive, and if perchance the weather was broken it was a nerve racking time for the owner, who tried to avail of every dry hour and all available manpower to get the crop saved. Such conditions prevailed when the Gunner prayed for his deliverance, from sheaves with thistles in them, scorching sun, and the distance that lay between him and a pint a porter to aid a raging thirst.

The field in question was con-acre (rented land) consisting or 'round five Irish acres. In modern parlance eight statute or three hectares. The soil was good but the drainage poor due to lack of maintenance of the deep drains that surrounded it. High thorn bushes with briers and brambles growing out from the butt were not a help to drying conditions. In present times, the field would be a must for tourists or for those following our past history, for it had the original potato ridges of famine times in it.

The man who rented the field was a local entrepreneur by the name of Ned Chamney. He had a truck for hire in the locality but had a nose for turning a pound in other projects. The prices for grain had risen during the war and had stayed high post war, hence his interest in the field. A shrewd operator he considered he was on a fair gamble. Old lea ground freshly broken, and this hadn't been ploughed in the memory of man, usually produced a good crop. Given half decent weather at harvest it was a case of winner all right! He even had an acre knocked off the original acreage to make up for loss of ground that lay under the briers and brambles that grew out from the boundary hedges when the bargain had been struck.

He sowed oats with a view to selling it into the various horse studs that were in the area, and it flourished from the moment the first green shoots peeked above the ground. By harvest time it looked a bumper crop, straw four feet high with a good head of grain. The field had also produced an equally good crop of thistles. It was cut with a binder and stooked. The man on the binder said he was tired putting balls of twine into the twine box there were so many sheaves. All that was needed now was a week or so to let it ripen in the stooks then stack it. Once in stacks it was pretty safe weather wise.

They were hardly out of the field when the weather broke. It rained and rained and them rained some more. Sheets of it came down followed by high winds, which blew stooks down like skittles in bowling alley. The hollows either side of the old potato ridges filled up and the water sat there for it had nowhere to go; the main ditches blocked tight from years of neglect. The main storms cleared and the weather rose up into the worst possible conditions, blasts of hot sunshine followed by torrential thundershowers. Nightmare weather for anyone trying to get their harvest saved.

Ned waited and watched and after a few fair to middlin' days he made a move. Those battered stooks had to be straightened up somehow and the ones in the furrows moved onto the ridges to get them out of the water, which stubbornly refused to go away. He needed extra help so getting into his car he headed for the Job Centre in the local town, Kilcullen. In those days Job Centres was the windowsill of a pub in any rural area where the unemployed seeking work and the unemployed not seeking work (local loafers) hung out. It was a step up from the hiring fairs of ancient times but not so sophisticated as today's agencies. There were always a couple of early birds, those waiting to hear the rattle of the bolt on the Bar door signifying opening time, and then they could nip in and get the hair of the dog! By noon the full complement had gathered. Corner boys they were called, which was not a fair description, for manys the good man waited there hoping to land a day's work and the chance to earn a few bob in very hard times. Once the choice seats of the window sill were taken up the rest stood around, gossiping, swapping yarns, and making comment on the passing traffic, which consisted of the odd motor car, horses and carts, ponies and traps, and lots of folk on bikes. The pub in question, the Hide Out, was a corner site and that was a bonus for there were two windowsills, therefore traffic could be watched from all directions. It was also on top of a steep rise in the main street and manys the ribald comment passed between cyclist and loafer if the cyclist was pushing hard to get to the top.

"Lie on her Peter".

"Go on, give her Katie Barry."

"Jasus, if ya had her headed t'other way you'd take off."

These jibs were reciprocated with equal vulgarity.

"G'wanne ya wasters, thinkin' about work i'd frightened da shite in ya."

Women cyclists didn't escape either.

"Hey Molly, yer petticoat is showin'."

"Well make da most ive it, for tis all ye'll see," would come the tart reply.

On this particular morning the Gunner Ryan stood with the bunch. He'd been one of the early birds and now had his backside resting on the windowsill letting a couple of pints settle on his stomach. Rooting in the top pocket of his fatigue jacket he pulled out a half Woodbine cigarette and cupping his hands 'round a match in that well known fashion of the outdoor man he lit up. Exhaling slowly he crossed his legs. In spite of his outward composure he was doing some concentrated thinking, for all that was left in his trouser pocket was four old tossers (pence). To die of starvation was one thing; to die of thirst was the ultimate agony. There wasn't a make to be had in the town. He'd got the room ready for the travelling barber who came every Saturday, rolled out offal barrels for the butcher, and stacked some timber in the hardware premises plus cleared out empties from the pub. There was nothing stirring. He was going through a list of names in his head wondering which one of them he could put the squeeze on to tide him over when Ned drove up. "I need a few hardy men," he called out airily. Three men stepped towards the car immediately. "You've come to the right spot Boss," replied one. It was make or brake time for the Gunner. Desperate circumstances call for desperate measures; he followed the three men into the car!

Hotter than hell was the only way to describe that field. Not a breath of air stirred, the high hedges saw to that, and the sun blazed down mercilessly on the workers who pulled on the heavy wet sheaves lifting them up onto the ridges setting six sheaves to a stook. Every so often they stopped to pick thistle thorns out of their hands for each sheaf had its complement of thistles. Constantly rubbing their forearms across their brows to wipe away the stinging sweat before it reached their eyes, they kept going. All 'round were inky blue black clouds, thunder rolled and rumbled in the nearby hills, t'would be a miracle if the weather held. T'was a miracle the Gunner wasn't anxious to witness. The pints had long since died in him and a couple a mugs of scalding sweet tea had only revived him temporarily. He began to wonder if this day was some sort of penance on him. The nuns had taught him in his brief school years that God was sometimes a wrathful God, and he had no doubt now that between the sweat and thistle thorns the full wrath of God was upon him. If Our Lady got a hint would she intercede for him, he wondered.

The inky black clouds got nearer and the sun took a rest. Suddenly a flash of lightning light up the sky followed immediately by a crash of thunder which rolled and rumbled on and on towards the distance hills. Everyone dashed for shelter to the hedge for they could hear it coming. That thunder shower hiss, which is heard a minute or so before the shower proper arrives. The hiss became a roar of falling rain as the first big drops fell, then, lo and behold, the sun peeped out from behind the black cloud that carried it. It bucketed down in the adjoining field and beyond, but apart from the first few drops, not another one fell in that furnace of a field. The men moved out from the hedge, glanced at the clearing sky and carried on stooking. For the Gunner it was the last straw. Stepping out from the shelter of the hedge he gazed heavenwards, "Holy sufferin' lovin' Mother a Jasus," he implored, "tis a whore entirely, for 'tis rainin' all over Ireland and it won't rain here!

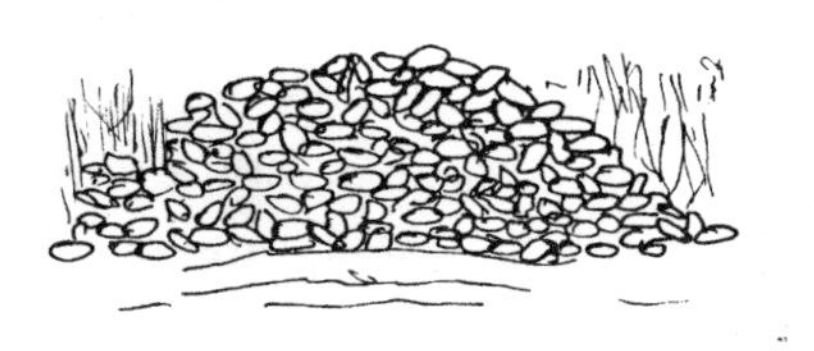

Chapter 25
The Campaign

There are a few interesting facts to be found in a book written by Michael Foy in 1976 entitled The Sugar Industry in Ireland. For example, Irish citizens were transported as slaves to the sugar cane fields of Barbados a year after Cromwell sacked Drogheda and that was as long ago as 1650. In 1768 Irish slaves planned a sugar rebellion in Montserrat. Could that have been the forerunner of today's modern strike? Napoleon apparently had an interest in sugar for political reasons. So you can see that sugar goes back a long way, even as far back as 510 BC when Darius the Persian leader and his troops came across it on the banks of the river Indus. They called it 'the reeds that produced sugar without bees'. Honey I guess was its rival. The first attempt to establish a sugar beet industry in Ireland was the erection of a factory at Mountmellick by the Royal Irish Beet Root Sugar Company in 1851. It folded in 1862. The first sugar factory with government backing was established at Carlow: Mallow, Thurles, and Tuam were to follow.

But that was then. In the mid thirties, Father, being a progressive sort of man decided to have a go at growing sugar beet. One had to apply for a contract and I think his first contract was for five acres. It was grown at the top of the Hillfield; the rest of the fifteen acres was planted with turnips, mangels, and potatoes, all for yard and house consumption. He had a good reason for planting the beet at the top of the field for it bordered the public road which at the time was the usual place to dump beet awaiting delivery to the factory. No one gave any thought to the muck and clay that plastered the road in wet times, or bothered about traffic hold up when a truck was being loaded! Two, three, and with a bit of luck, four men with strong backs fired the beet into the truck with six tined forks. These forks were designed specially for beet handling, each tine having a nodule at the end to prevent damage to the beet. Eight to ten tons was considered a good truckload, and depending on manpower took about an hour to load. Thirty tons is about average in present times.

There's no comparison between the handling of sugar beet thirty or forty years ago with todays methods. Today's beet field is ploughed, manured, sprayed, sown and lifted, mechanically. A beet harvester moves up and down the drills effortlessly, spewing the beets into a trailer that moves alongside. The trailer filled it heads for the clamp, a designated spot, tips its load and heads back for another one. An elevator or front loader fills the truck. Such is progress, and anyone who has ever worked in a root field on a cold miserable winters day would say, "Thank God"

From time immemorial roots have been grown in Ireland. Turnips, mangels, and potatoes were the staples, but the arrival of the sugar beet crop awoke parts of rural Ireland, especially those parts near where a factory had been erected. That's not to say that beet growing took off like wildfire. Farmers the world over are a cautious lot, and Irish farmers equally so. "Let's see how the other Lad is doin'. "Let the other Lad be the trend setter." Politics also took a hand. Slavery had long since been abolished, and cane sugar from the West Indies, once grown for practically free found a competitor in sugar beet. The money moguls trading in sugar futures on the London Stock Exchange, ladies gossiping over a cup of afternoon tea on the virtues of cane versus beet, and how it might affect the baking of bread or scones, all had a bearing on the progress of sugar beet growing in Europe and Ireland was a part of Europe. Money is the bottom line with all products, and farmers were quick to realise that return per acre is what counts. The growing of sugar beet progressed!

For reasons unknown to me the harvesting of sugar beet became known as "The Campaign" The word campaign, denotes a war or battle, and battle it was. Battle to get the crop out before the weather broke, before the factory closed, and most important of all, the battle to get it out before the neighbour! In the Fall of the year and if you lived in the Carlow area where the biggest factory was, the conversation in pub, farmyard, or headland, was centred around "The Campaign." "What ar'ya at." "Oh. We're at da beaaat" If you lived near Mallow in Co Cork it would sound like this, "What are ye at?" "Oh we've starrrated de beeeet." It was important to get all roots harvested and stored safely before winter set in, but there's no doubt the "Campaign" overshadowed all. The Campaign hasn't gone away but modern methods have taken some of the buzz out of it.

Up our way and thirty miles from the factory at Carlow the "Campaign" didn't take on the same significance. We were grazier's country. Cattle, horses, and sheep took precedence. A man might stay up most of the night watching a cow due to calve or a mare to foal, or a sheep about to lamb, but ask him to pull or crown beet was tantamount to insulting him. Beet pullers came from somewhere else, we were stockmen. This attitude caused a minor hick up to Father's ambition to be a beet grower but he got over it in his own inimitable way. His first workforce was made up of rabbit trappers (professional and poacher) and the odd fellow who would do a few hours just to keep from starving. The trouble with this arrangement was that they worked the hours that suited them, not Fathers. With the days getting shorter and factory closing date looming up he made his move. He bought a car trailer with sides attached and headed for the job centre in Castledermot—'Copes corner'. The Campaign was winding up south of us and with Christmas round the corner men stood around hoping to get a few days work He had no trouble filling the car and trailer. In no time flat the beet moved from the field to the pile on the roadside. He was a noted man for getting work done faster than anyone else. This was achieved by a simple method. The trick was to pick a good worker and put him in a position where others had to keep up. In other words a pacesetter. Sometimes he himself took on the task. He would start the day working with the men then leave after a while, he and they knowing full well how much could be accomplished in such an such a time.

On one occasion this method backfired. A gang of men were pulling beet a pacesetter among them. Arriving in the field round noon to see how things were progressing he noted the pacesetter well ahead of the posse. Before passing comment to the others he walked the drill that the pacesetter was working on and soon saw the reason for the man's remarkable progress. Like any job there is an art form to pulling beet simple and all as it looks. You grab a beet in either hand from the drill either side of you, bang them together to knock off surplus clay then lay them down and grab two more. This joker was pulling and dropping making no effort to knock the clay off. When remonstrated by Father he replied with typical Irish wit, "Jasus Boss, de ya want me to squeeze the sugar out of 'em fer ya? A bit if wit, the odd prank, helped to alleviate the drudgery on a lot of farm jobs, and nowhere was it most needed then in a root field.

Bureaucracy also played its part when beet was moved from farm to factory for each load needed a movement permit, or 'docket' as it was known colloquially. The following vexatious tale tells of what happens when bureaucracy overrules logic. A local lorry man, Noel Shirley, splashed out and purchased a brand new Ford tractor unit and trailer to match. His was the first artic (articulated) truck in the county. Noel handled all farm produce and in the autumn was busily engaged moving sugar beet from farm to factory. He pulled over the factory scales one day and found the scales not up to the job. Its maximum weighing abilities was fifteen tons. There was nothing for it only pull over to one side where he and his helper humped off the excess beet. That done, he was back on the scales, and this time, all was ok; the load was under fifteen tons. Next move was to the 'washer' where the load was washed out by power hose, then back to load up the excess beet and have it weighed. It weighed three and a half tons and it was at this stage that the full weight of bureaucracy was applied. The three and a half tons was considered by the powers to be, a separate load, therefore needing a separate movement permit (docket). Logic and Noel considered it part of the load he had first arrived with. Argument took place and tempers flared but to no avail, there was nothing for it but to return the three and a half tons to the place from whence it came, the farmer's yard. He wasn't best pleased either. Four times that miserable load was handled which only goes to prove that bureaucracy and logic are not bedfellows!

All roots are lifted in the autumn or early winter and at that time of year the sun is not shining on your back as you move down the drill bent over, struggling to wrench the unyielding root from its comfortable bed! It was a backbreaking, muscle aching job. Depending on which crop you were working on there was a distinction as to what you were doing. Beet was crowned, turnips were snagged and mangels were wrung. It all meant one and the same thing. You were separating the tops or leaves from the root with back breaking effort. Beet and turnips were done with a knife, mangel leaves removed by hand. When you got to the headland or end of drill a lot of stretching was done to try and get the kink out of your back. Of the three crops to be pulled mangels were the pits. They were softer than beet or turnips and it was sacrilege to use a knife on them. They would bleed, was the perceived thinking at the time, so having wrestled it out of the ground you then had to wrestle the leaves from the root with bare hands. The welts that grew between your first finger and thumb would do justice to a rhinoceros hide!

Facing into a field of roots after a nights frost, or worse, a spill of rain was a daunting task. With the leaves meeting across the drills you didn't travel too far before you were wet from arse to elbow. To help alleviate the situation you wore sacking wrapped 'round your knees tied on with binder twine. Used 2cwt super-phosphate sacks were in great demand. They were made of jute. One sack cut in two was the real wheat, a half for each leg. By lunch time there'd be half a cwt of clay stuck to them and you took them off to dry out a bit, but mostly I think to relieve yourself of the weight.

The good old times? Ask someone who has ever worked in a root field on a cold, miserable, winter's day!

Chapter 26

T'will Do Well Enough

I remember some years ago getting for a Xmas present a book of cartoons by that famous cartoonist Giles, long since dead. It was his Xmas edition and was one of the best presents I got at that time, for I had only to flick through it and it had me rolling with laughter. However, the one that I enjoyed the most and has stayed with me down through the years was the centre page. Actually it was two cartoons about the same subject. On the left page was a drawing of an immaculately dressed man in hunting dress on an immaculately turned out horse leaning over in the saddle and opening an immaculately hung gate. The caption read "An English Hunting Gate". On the right hand page the drawing consisted of two large stone gate piers, a large pile of stones in the gap between the piers, a bed end jammed into the stones on one side and a length of pole stuck in the other end. The same immaculately dressed huntsman on the same immaculately turned out horse was whipping him half way up the pile of stones, the horse unable to make up his mind whether to try jumping the pile or keep on scrambling. The caption for this cartoon was,—you've probably guessed it, "An Irish Hunting Gate."

That cartoon has remanded indelibly printed on my mind, and often makes me wonder why we Irish are so inclined to do a half- arsed job on some project, when a bit of extra effort would insure a more lasting effect and look more pleasing to the eye, especially where it involves fencing, or gate hanging in particular. Just take a drive on any Irish road, you may not see an exact replica of the cartoon I've described, but you'll see a variation on the same theme.

The lazy Irish, a shiftless lot? How often we've all heard these remarks passed. I'm not here to pass judgement on the rights or wrongs of those comments; I'll leave that to the specialists in that field, and just say "If the cap fits"! My father, God rest the Man, had a saying for situations that involved a quick fix, "We'll do it up good later." Later, could mean after dinner, tomorrow, next week, next year, but he could not be described as either lazy or shiftless. Careless maybe, for he was always two steps ahead of himself, and everybody else for that matter when it came to getting work done.

To get back to the gate hanging situation, there are many and varied reasons for the half hung gate or not hung at all gate, which is the one just slapped up against the hanging post and tied to it with a piece of barbed wire or baling twine (the farmers friend). To be fair, a newly strung fence line or hedge with gateway placed somewhere along it is usually a good and complete job whether it was done yesterday or a hundred years ago. It must also be remembered that a gate fixing operation is always considered a fill in job for an hour or so, until the dew dries off hay before turning it, or off the field of grain before starting to cut, or until all stock is fed and looked after in winter time. As I've already said an original fence or gateway was always correct and proper, but the arrival of the big machine is one of the reasons for the dilapidated look on some of our gateways today. Gates that were originally eight feet wide were extended to nine, ten, twelve on up to fifteen or twenty feet today, to make room for bigger and bigger machines to manoeuvre through. The original piers were probably granite or stone built and then came the widening operation. Knock down one of the piers was the easiest option if not already nudged, or knocked by some machine with a careless operator. To re-erect a stone pier is a slow time consuming job and requires some skill. The good intention is to rebuild someday, but in the meantime a bit of a post will get you by, and as you haven't yet got that new wider gate sure a bed end or pallet (modern day fixit wonder) will do. A couple of poles criss-crossed will also get you by.

Meanwhile, the dew has dried off the hay/ grain, get at it, the sun don't shine forever, so the good intention gets put on the back burner and anyways there is another fill in job to be done elsewhere, and the job you set out to do, to make way for a wider machine is complete, the tidying up can be done later. Famous last words! The fact that it takes three times longer to untwist barbed wire, open baler twine knots and drag a pallet or bed-end to get the "new gate" open, rather than hang it properly in the first place doesn't seem to enter into the equation. Mind you there is a certain logic and often a good reason for the gateway with the pile of stones dumped in the middle. There are times, due to some re-planning that the original position of the gateway has become obsolete and sits there forlorn and neglected looking. Now practically all farms have a stone problem and from time to time these stones are picked off tillage fields. Once you have your horse cart or tractor trailer filled with the above commodity you have to have someplace to put them. No use tipping them into a ditch, you'll probably block a watercourse, and if at some future date you want them for fill under concrete, you'll have an awkward time re-loading. A convenient place to dump them is what you are seeking and where better than between those stone gate piers that are lying idle. Who knows, between the time you put them there and when you get 'round to needing them you'll probably have graduated to a tractor with front -end loader! These are just a couple of reasons for the gate artistry we have in this country Maybe its pure fantasy on my part but fantasy is as good a reason as any, when it comes to explaining the mosaics of gates and gateways we see in rural Ireland.

A wire fence or hedge is another opportunity for the quick fix artist to display his mental abilities. A hole in a thorn hedge where sheep are breaking out is a piece of cake. Cut a few bushes at the top of the hedge and stuff them into the bottom where the animals are getting through. Cut and push you could say, but it only encourages the sheep to move further along the hedge and seek or make another hole, and they will for sure! In desperation and a week or two later a roll of sheep wire is purchased and strung up in proper fashion. A loose strand or two in a wire fence is no problem to the mental resources of Mr Quick-Fix. The same loose strand of wire seems to act like a magnet to a nosy animal that'll find it, poke his head through and graze the other side. He'll keep stretching for fresh grazing and soon has another strand loosened. Another bit of a push and he's out the other side. A repair job is needed.

Now, there are three ways of doing a job. The right way, the wrong way, or the quick way, tho' my Father had a variation on that one. He always said, there was the right way, the wrong way, and his way! The quick way in not necessarily the wrong way. It can get you out of a hobble if something more important is pending, but when it becomes the permanent way then trouble looms up at a future date and always strikes when busy at something else, such as harvesting on a fine day, or on a Sunday when you're sitting with your feet up looking at a football match, or worse, gone to the match! There's nothing to dissipate a couple a pints or your bon-homie quicker, than an irate red-faced wife greeting you at the door, with the news that she has spent the last hour trying to get the cattle out of the barley or neighbours. Both she and the dog look exhausted, and she doesn't have to tell you where they broke out! Your mind immediately focuses on that quick fix job you did a few days ago and have never got back to it. When you arrive at the scene of the break out you are very sober. Miniature carbon copies of the Normandy Landings greet you. Wire twisted and tangled, fence posts pulled and broken, the quick fix job that took you about ten minutes, has developed into a half days work or more.

So how was the quick fix job accomplished? Very simple, just place the handle of the hammer, or if you have a short length of iron bar the better, along the loose wire and twist a loop on it. There you are your strand of loose wire now as tight as a fiddle string. A day or two later the nosy animal that first poked his head through to graze on the other side (the grass is always greener on the other side) tries again. This time it takes a little longer and a bit of ingenuity on his part. Turning his head sideways he shoves it through and finds a bare patch, because he'd grazed that bit last try. Now he has to try harder, so he gets his shoulder to the wire and pushes to reach that fresh lush bit. The inevitable happens, the wire snaps at the twist and your man is through to the far side grazing in comfort. Naturally his pals get interested and go to investigate, and soon the whole herd is through. They don't pay much attention to protocol and their manners leave much to be desired as they push and shove one another through the gap in their haste to try out new pastures. The whole place is a mess, and the match post mortem with a few pals and a few pints fades from your memory as you grind your teeth and get stuck in.

There are a couple of other reasons or should they be called excuses for the "do it up good later," thinking. Farming in older times was mixed, a bit of everything was grown or reared Today we are in the specialist field; therefore one can focus solely on that particular field. In mixed farming one had to set one's mind in several different directions every day one got up. Not an easy task you must agree, hence the quick switch from fence repairs to haying or harvesting within a short space of time. Too many irons in the fire. Another reason / excuse was lashings of help 'round the place. On medium to large farms help would consist of three or four and up to twelve men on each place. On small holdings when a major task needing help was taking place i.e. spud picking, the neighbours pitched in, so no one bothered much about simplifying the job at hand, or tidying up after the job was finished. The perceived thinking being, sure someone else will do it.

Nowhere was this more exemplified than in the handling and sorting of livestock. The T. B. Eradication Scheme started in the mid fifties by the Dept of Agriculture, and looking like it will run on to the mid fifties in the next century, hasn't yet achieved it's objective of eliminating T. B. in our livestock, but it has achieved an objective of sorts. It made farmers erect proper penning facilities for what was once a time consuming job, the handling and sorting of livestock, even if some of the penning erected leaves much to be desired. An iron twelve foot gate with a couple of stakes propping it up running parallel to a stone wall is the basic model. It improves from there in various shapes and sizes right up to the deluxe models, holding pens, sorting pens, loading bays and race / shute. In the times I speak of, the best holding and sorting pen available was the public road. Sometimes an effort was made to sort in the corner of a field; it all depended on how much help was available. A couple of young lads, your own or the neighbours to act as dogs were necessary! But even with help available the public road was still the best. It was narrow for a start, so one man standing between two lots of animals was able to keep them apart and at the same time let up or down the one or ones being sorted. Road traffic was light, and if per chance a vehicle came along he bided his time, and if he were a neighbour he got out to give a hand to the proceedings, helping to speed things up. If loading cattle into a truck the public road was still the best place. The trucker pulled tight to the hedge and the cattle were coaxed along to the ramp. Usually, everything went just fine, but if one broke through the human barrier surrounding him all hell broke loose, for a galloping animal with an open road stretching before him had a number of options. He could keep going, and in doing so test the very best of sprinters or long distance runners.

The trick was for someone, usually the fittest, to squeeze through the hedge into the adjoining field and try to keep pace and eventually overtake the fugitive. The other option the runaway could take was to jump into the adjacent fields on the right or left of him and join up with the neighbours stock. This in turn caused great excitement among the neighbour's animals who chased the guest 'round and 'round the field pucking and cavorting at him and at each other. Back at base camp, the truck at the edge of the road, help was dispatched to help the original chaser. If luck was against you, and it usually was in such situations, thère're be no gate in the neighbours field leading onto the road where your animal had chosen to jump into. The only option was to round up all and head for the nearest gate leading back onto the road, which could entail a lengthy journey over a number of fields, and you had to watch out for the place where he had originally jumped in for it was on the cards he would try again. This sort of interlude made it very difficult to put a precise time on destination arrival, and very often if time was of the essence the damned animal was left there and got home at some future date.

Help was also available if an animal got sick or lame. Again, the whole lot were got in from the field, and the one needing attention run into an outhouse there to be chased around until caught. There're be one person swinging out of his nose, one out of his tail, and a third administering to his wants. With all this help around there was no onus on a farmer to improve his present arrangements. Why go to expense setting up handling facilities that at most would only be used a few times a year when a couple of young lads with their tongues hanging out for an hour or so would cost next to nothing or nothing at all!

Today's farmers are mostly one man operators except for the very large ones, and nothing concentrates the mind better than when you have to do the job yourself. Simplicity and ease of operation is much to the forefront when planning. No one is coming behind to tidy up after you, and where would you get a couple of young lads now- a- days to work for next to nothing! Nevertheless, there is still evidence about to show that we haven't completely lost the quick fix mental attitude or of our ability to put things on the long finger. Next time you take a drive, and are watching out for some of our quaint gateways complete with pile of stones, keep a lookout for some very expensive pieces of equipment such as £100,000 combines sitting in gateways and fields, unclean and untouched since the last field was cut the previous harvest. I suppose we can put it all down to an attitude of mind. A gate stuck here, a hurdle placed there on a temporary basis, sure t'will do well enough!

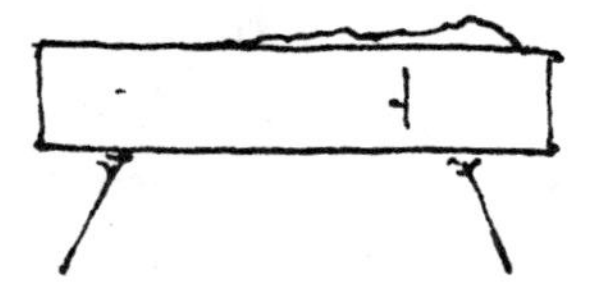

Chapter 27
The Wake

One cannot live in rural Ireland for most of one's life and not give a mention about The Wake! As you grow older you do achieve an attendance record of sorts by going to funerals. That is if you live in Ireland, for we are an inveterate nation of funeral goers especially if you belong to the political or auctioneering classes. Its known in those trade circles as "keeping an eye to business"; the touch of reverence goes down well and doesn't do any harm at all! As one grows older your attendance record rises, and cynical thought, one could be forgiven for thinking that you just might be building an attendance bank for your own. But we are an emotional and forgiving people on such sad occasions, and are prepared to let bygones be bygones. As the line in the song goes, "a mane auld craythur when alive, a dacent man when dead." I heard a couple of old timers at a funeral recently, yes I'm building my own bank; it went something like this,—"How's she goin Tom.?" "Not so bad, thank God, I'm still above ground, but ya know, I find I'm goin to more funerals than weddings these times." Came the tart reply, "Ya hav'ta get invited to a weddin'.

All joking aside, there is still in Ireland an awe and reverence for the dead. We haven't yet succumbed to the American way of dying where the offers you get from funeral parlours are similar to supermarket offers minus the discount. Brand X's wares are superior to all other brands, better box, softer than soft lining, a good paint job (on the corpse) and all offered in a saccharine cloying voice accompanied by suitable woe be gone music that would encourage you to throw up if there was a last dying gasp left in you. The hard sell, offered in embalming tones to lure you into the parlour though not necessarily into heaven.

Mind you, in subtle ways there's a touch of commercialism creeping into Irish funerals. We're in the nuclear family age now and everything has to be streamlined and efficient and funerals are not exempted. Down through the years in rural Ireland most funerals left from the house: the home of the deceased, after a proper wake, and after the burial friends and neighbours returned to the house for a bite to eat and drink and to sustain the bereaved. I guess the only exception to this was when one died in hospital and then the funeral started from the hospital mortuary usually passing by the house on the way to church or graveyard. Nowadays, there's a slight change. Somebody dies and the priest doctor and undertaker; in that order are called. The work of the first two completed the undertaker arrives and takes over, and the body is removed to the funeral parlour where those wishing to pay their respects can call. Burial next day after funeral service or whenever suitable, and all back to local hotel for tea and sandwiches. A neat, efficient, and well conducted operation and well suited to the pace of life to day.

So what has happened to the traditional Irish wake? Has modern times consigned it to history? No, not around these parts anyway; you could say it's making a comeback. Deceased bodies are being taken from hospitals and brought back to the house there to receive due reverence, in other words waked. Time and history has a way of obscuring fact from fiction, and over the years quare stories are told of the happenings at wakes Singing and dancing, ribald stories told, the corpse sitting up in the coffin freighting the life out of those sitting around it. Are all these shannigians attributed to wakes true or false? Mostly false, but with a certain element of truth. A couple a pints a porter, a whiskey, or maybe a nip of the rale stuff can transform any party be it a wedding or a wake, and there's always jokes and jokers in attendance at either. Practical jokes were played. If the house was small, containing only one chimney, it was not unknown for someone to climb up onto the roof and throw a wet sack over it smoking out all below in double quick time. Not only are we Irish a spiritual people we are also a superstitious lot. Its hard to find someone who has actually seen a banshee, its even harder to find someone who will deny her existence. Therefore, if you find yourself due to lack of space in the house, standing out in an Irish haggard on a dark night at a wake and you hear a rattle going on behind a haystack you won't be in any rush to suss out the cause, but you'll certainly give an opinion on it, and so will everyone else around you. A drink or two taken, add in a bit of Irish imagination and the rattle will turn into Auld Nick himself coming for the soul of the departed. Everyone down on their knees praying for the soul of the departed. Auld Nick of course is a couple of tin cans tied together and fixed to the back of the haystack, a long length of twine running out through the haggard ditch and at the back of the ditch joker man himself, giving it the odd chuck now and again. There's one in every parish!!

There was a certain logic or order to wakes in olden times

They could be divided into two parts. The first part was to offer support and condolences to the bereaved. The support being mostly in the form of food, and the odd bottle slipped quietly unto the sideboard or dresser, for large quantities were needed. Neighbours, friends, and relations from far and near helped out. After the burial the second part clicked in, when a more light hearted atmosphere prevailed. The same stories were told and re-told, and maybe added to, some of them being about the deceased, their good qualities and attributes for rarely does one speak ill of the dead. The whole scene was to try and lighten the grief and burden of those who were bereaved, and let them see that life must go on. Everyone was a homespun psychologist before psychology was heard of. Certain customs were observed, in those times. New clay pipes plug tobacco and snuff (some women took snuff) were laid out on a table mostly for the benefit of those who were going to sit up all night with the corpse. There was a colour scheme also. The corpse was dressed in a habit or shroud, the colour brown indicated an old person, white was for someone young or single, and blue was I suppose somewhere in between. In the days before motor hearses the horses drawing the hearse wore plumes fixed to their bridles carrying the colours which indicated the status of the deceased And before horse drawn hearses? Well, four strong men replaced along the way by four more and so on until the final destination was arrived at carried the corpse manually. Bearers, they were called, and it was important that they were of equal height for a short fellow on the team could find most of the weight on his shoulders.

And so we get back to today's times. I mean no disrespect to funeral parlours or mortuaries, for I have observed how their staff moves around helping confused and bereaved people in a quiet and unobtrusive way. But by the very nature of their work they turn friends and neighbours into spectators. If you want to be a spectator you can go to a football match. Death is a very sombre time but it gives friends and neighbours an opportunity to express their true worth and to show their appreciation of the deceased by doing any hands turn asked of them Watching undertakers and hotel staff doing all that's necessary leaves them with a feeling of helplessness. That is why I for one am glad to see and hear of the return of the wake. Thank God, we haven't yet traipsed off to Brussels or Washington to find out how to run an Irish funeral. An E C directive or Washington edict is the last thing we need on such a sensitive matter. I'd like to go on with this story but you must excuse me, I have to go to a funeral. Don't forget to wake me!

Chapter 28
Idle Thoughts

I sit here and reflect on forty odd years spent on the land. Farming, watching farming, talking farming. The past, the present. The good years, the bad years. The pros and cons. Prices, good and bad. Returns per acre v returns per animal. Grass v cereals. Urban v rural. The drift from the land. Necessary appendages to farming, vets, bank managers, accountants, feed and seed merchants. Unnecessary, bureaucrats (all kinds), sales reps, the tax man! Burdens on farmers, forms to be filled out, forms to be tossed in the fire. With the arrival of soft tissue toilet paper there's no further use for them! The list of topics seems endless, and I suppose the biggest of all is the weather which will keep a conversation going like nothing else. "Looks like rain". "Will it freeze.?" "A week's fine weather wouldn't do a bit a harm". When two rural folk meet the greeting is always the same. "Fine day, thank God", or "Isn't that a real hoor of a day". It all depends in which field you want the weather in. The roots are wilting for a sup-a-rain, and the best hay you ever made is in the field beside them.

There's no doubt, but the weather is the most important factor in agricultural circles. Pity for all them Brussels bureaucrats, shuffling pieces of paper, gazing into their computer screens, dreaming up edicts, decrees and directives, working out tonnage's and percentages, getting out piles of statistics, then along comes Mother Nature with a Force 10 gale or a merciless sun for weeks on end and in the words of the Poet, "The best laid schemes o' mice an' men gang aft a-gley."

There's another appendage tacked on to farmer's backs today that has doubtful use. The economic report. Your mailman arrives and hands you a bunch of letters, three of them bills, one a letter from a distant relative in Australia/America and a large long white envelope containing the very latest up to date economic report, by a leading economist no less, on how things were last year or the year before. Yesterday's news, it might as well tell you what went on in the year of dot! It's all tied in to possibilities for the current year, plus or minus, give or take, (no mention of a Hurricane, or a heatwave on the way.) The only possibility that holds any interest for a farmer is, will it possibly rain to night on those grass seeds he sowed to day, or will the sun possibly shine on the field of hay he turned to day and hopes to bale tomorrow. A farmer has to be very discerning with his mail these days. The bills are stacked with all the others to be put on the long finger payment system, the distant relative one is read to see how he/she is getting on, and the economic report goes to the stick box to help light the fire. Unless you are a history buff, the thing to do is to glance through it and pick up a few relevant points, these will enable you to argue like hell in a pub or mart sometime later, on how things were last year. It doesn't matter a damn that every other farmer in the argument got the same report, with a bit of luck you'll be the only one who's glanced through it.

Stress, now there's another factor we have to deal with to day. It's in the workforce, schools and colleges, and sure I suppose it has to be in farming. When did it arrive? Where did it come from? Was it always there? How does it affect you when the sun is blazing down and you want rain, or it's pissing out of the heavens and you want sunshine? There's an old saying that says, "If you meet a young lad goin' the road, give him a kick in the arse, he's either coming from mischief or goin' to it." Give him a kick in the arse to day and you'll end up in court with irate parents screaming to have you hung up or sent down for life. Could you claim stress? "Due to poor weather conditions Me Lord I got this sudden urge." I don't know about years ago. I guess they were around, but today you could bring your Shrink with you into court. With a Shrink and solicitor you might have a chance, and anyways standing between those two stalwarts you'd have the feel good factor. To day if you get in a rage, it's probably because your mother tripped over a straw and a hen picked her when she was carrying you. Years ago if you got in a rage it was probably because the tractor wouldn't start, or a ewe wouldn't sit still and you trying to shear her or pare her feet. You gave her a couple a thumps or shouted at the dog and felt better. What about that visit to your bank manager in response to his letter as to how he'd like to see you sometime soon, and paying him for the privilege. That's a laugh, that one. If it wasn't for the information you give him he wouldn't be in a position to make a decision. If you go to a doctor for information as to your well being, you'll get a bill for sure. Information costs money these days, why give yours away for free. If you're in a bad humour due to weather conditions and can't get on with what you planned, is that stress? But lo and behold, something always turns up on those occasions. Instead of making hay as planned you hike off to the mart with a few bullocks or lambs and get a rattling good price, suddenly the sun is shining, metaphorically speaking anyway! I'm not competent enough to write on this subject, so I'll leave that to the experts, but a last word on it.

Maybe it's working with the land, animals and weather, and all their quirky ways (good and bad) that keeps a farmer in balance and leaves the stress to the other fella whoever he may be.

I waffle on: yes farmers have left the hob-nailed boots behind and joined the Doc Martin age, tho' the wellie is still the preferred footwear for those special kinds of days. We belong to the consumer group now, tho' we were never looked upon as needing food and clothes like everyone else. I suppose wearing all those superphosphate and grain sacks over our shoulders to keep out the weather instead of coats, gave people that opinion. Once upon a time you stuck your head under a cow and got milk for the day, or dug a bucket a spuds in the garden for the dinner. Now he/she walk up and down the supermarket aisles filling their trolley same as everyone else. A 2.5 Kg of spuds, a box of easy spread, and a couple a cartons of milk. Mind you, he could have 50 or 60 cows going through the milking parlour back home, but they're designated to keep the cash flow flowing,

Now there's another matter that should be addressed forthwith. You get your "End of year Tax Return form," the Inspector informing you to fill in your name and address (block capitals) and all your dependants. In small print a list of suggested dependants: spouse, children under 18, an ailing mother-in-law. Is the man for real? One of these days I'll send in a full list, and shouldn't ever have to pay a red cent ever again. Dependants! the list is endless: sales reps, insurance agents, mart personnel, livestock and fertiliser haulers, hardware and grain merchants, meat factory workers, vets, bank managers and accountants, including the Inspector himself Get that lot off your back and the garden could be rosy, maybe save a bob or two for that perpetual rainy day. There's no doubt, but the Tax man and the farmer look at financial situations from a different prospective, and the following tale may describe the difference. When farmers came into the tax net way back in the seventies this particular farmer, we'll call him Ned, collected up those little brown envelopes with the window in them and Inspector of Taxes stamped on them. When the pile got big he used them for getting the fire going in the mornings. Down in the pub one night he was persuaded by his farming friends to do something about it. "These revenue fellas don't go away," was the advice given, "and sooner or later they'll catch up with ye". The amount due was around £30,000. Ned took the bull by the horns and next day headed for the Revenue office. "Is the Boss in", he enquired at reception. "Who shall I say is calling and do you have an appointment" the receptionist asked, smiling sweetly at him. "Don't trouble yer self" sez Ned, brushing by her and pushed open the door that led into the inner sanctum. "Are ye da Boss?" he asked of the fellow sitting behind a large desk, "I owe ye a few bob, sure I'll give it to ye now". He pulled a large wad of dough from a back pocket. The Boss didn't bat an eye, enquired of his name and opened a large ledger. "Ah yes, here you are, the sum outstanding is £30,000 plus interest." Ned slapped the wad on the desk. "There's 15 grand there, take it or leave it". A bird in the hand was the Revenue mans thinking, and sure the rest would come eventually. Ned headed for the door. "Just a moment Sir" says the Boss, "we have to enter this amount in our ledger and issue you a receipt" Ned stood rooted to the floor, perplexity written all over his face. "Cripes", sez he, "ya don't mane ta tell me dat you're puttin' dat through da books?" This sort of thinking does not apply solely to farmers!

Vets, they need a mention; they have to be a special case, a breed apart. Masochists, all of them. If they have the intelligence to study veterinary practice the same brains will get them into medical school. Same length of time studying, same cost. Opting for the vet college is where their brains leave them. Imagine having the choice of sitting on a bed chatting up a patient (female preferred) or standing at a cattle shute on a pissing wet day with your arm full stretch up a cow's rear end being pissed and scruttered on for the privilege. Or getting called out in the middle of the night and on arrival finding your patient down in the middle of a field. No arc lights, no nurse fussing over you handing you the necessities, the only lighting a torch flickering away at you, suffering from a poor connection or run down battery All farmers have a touch of the cute hoor in them, and will have done their own doctoring before calling in the vet, helps keep down expenses. A shot of this or that left over from last year, the use by date blanked out by a smear of marking fluid which indicates that the bottle of whatever was last used when branding lambs the previous summer. "T'will hardly do him any "rale" harm" is the wisdom. The vet in a crafty way has to find out what the animal did get and then praise the farmer for his astute diagnosis. The farmer is as happy as Larry, figuring he had him half cured and on the road to recovery even tho 'the animal maybe half dead. He only got the vet for a second opinion. Beats Banagher being a vet, I tell ya!

If you hear a car pull up to your door, don't answer it. Let the dog bark awhile. There's nothing to beat a good wicked dog about the place, or at least one who sounds like he might be. There's more of the second kind than the first. If you can manage a peep out the window without been seen, all the better. If you don't like the look of the geezer, sit tight, the dog will encourage him to move off. Nine out of ten cars coming to the door are of no benefit to farmers. It's usually someone trying to sell you something you don't want. If he's a smooth salesman you'll end up buying a sample to be put in the barn with all the other samples you've bought from time to time, half used them, and are now afraid to dump them because of all the warning signs on them. Worse still, it could be the neighbour who wants to borrow some piece of equipment and always leaves it back broken or something missing off it and swears blind it was that way when he got it.

Mind you, I think travelling salesmen are on the wane. It's the sound bite on T.V now, or worse still, that invite to a seminar .in your local hotel. Don't go. You'll spend a boring time listening to some bloke spoofing about the advantages of some new super-dooper user-friendly product that you cannot possibly do without if you wish to remain financially viable. You're itching for him to finish before the bar closes, (your only reason for going out in the first place), then it happens. Like a meeting in a mission hall where someone gets up and sings out "Praise the Lord" and in jig time the whole hall is on its feet praising the Lord, so to at your seminar. John Joe goes up and buys a 10 litre can of the wonder product and in no time at all a queue forms. Horror of horrors, the neighbour who borrows and wrecks your machinery is now at the head of the queue and you see him buying a 25 litre can. That does it, your not going to be bested by him, and you take a 25 litre plus a 10. Six months or a year later the wonder product is still resting against the back wall of the barn. You have plans to give it a try, soon.

When you get old and grumpy farmers meetings are to be avoided at all costs. You'll only be listening to some fella who has missed the last six meetings holding the floor for half the night (unless the chairman shoots him). His beef, and it's his only, is that he had a load of grain returned or an animal rejected at the factory, and he wants every farmer, not only in the room but in the whole country to row in behind him to go and subpoena the Minister of Agriculture to a court hearing. He'll go home thoroughly disgruntled and miss the next six meetings. So will you, if you have any sense.

'Nuff said. Farming has grown into a high-powered business, the big getting bigger, the small ones squeezed out, in spite of blatherings from respective governments about keeping people on the land. It's a world phenomenon, but two things won't change, the vagaries of the weather, and the farmer's outlook on life! It has been said, I don't know by whom, "That a farmer buys retail, sells wholesale, and pays the haulage both ways "I can't sum it up any better!